James Louttit

Leading Impactful Teams

Achieving Low-Stress Success in Project Management

DE GRUYTER

ISBN 978-3-11-126940-5
e-ISBN (PDF) 978-3-11-127114-9
e-ISBN (EPUB) 978-3-11-127166-8

Library of Congress Control Number: 2023946986

Bibliographic information published by the Deutsche Nationalbibliothek
The Deutsche Nationalbibliothek lists this publication in the Deutsche Nationalbibliografie; detailed bibliographic data are available on the internet at http://dnb.dnb.de.

Cover image: Hybert Design
Printing and binding: CPI books GmbH, Leck

www.degruyter.com

James Louttit

Leading Impactful Teams

Advance Praise for *Leading Impactful Teams*

"A strong, motivated and unified team is essential to delivering change, no matter what the circumstances. In *Leading Impactful Teams*, James Louttit sets out how to bring people with diverse talents and viewpoints together in an effective way and motivate them to achieve their full potential."

— **Roderick O'Gorman**, Minister for Children, Equality, Disability, Integration and Youth of Ireland

"James has compiled a really practical set of techniques and tools which will certainly guide project managers to effectively manage projects and achieve project delivery success. Particularly impactful is the focus on people; leading teams and managing stakeholder expectations, through the project lifecycle. This book is written in unambiguous and engaging language, making it accessible and relevant for all levels of project delivery experience."

— **Gillian Brennan**, Business Operations Divisional Manager, Enterprise Ireland

"Louttit is on a mission – to empower project managers to lead more impactful projects (and avoid burning out while doing so!). Chock-full of tips, tricks and memorable cartoons, Louttit has created an accessible field-guide for anyone that wants their projects to deliver more impact with less stress."

— **Alasdair Trotter**, Partner & Managing Director @ Innosight

"This book is more holistic than traditional project management books. It imparts the experience of living through projects, both good and bad, hopefully helping those embarking on the road to avoid the pitfalls."

— **Rosalyn Donnelly**, Head of IT at C&D Foods (ABP Group)

"The book eloquently describes how project managers are often in the office jungle trying to navigate egos and non-productive or non-cooperative behaviour in individuals and teams. James provides a practical and common sense utility belt of exercises to engage and encourage collaboration that can cut through all the dancing around on egg shells and allow people to get out the way of themselves to deliver a result. I also recommend drinking whatever James does in the morning to give you the energy to succeed!"

— **Alistair Cornish**, Founder at Arconomy, former CTO at Sniip

"This book is a treasure trove of off-the-shelf tips, tools and techniques for each stage of your project to help you deliver. My favourite is the SAVE technique. It combines some amazing design thinking techniques with great output of execution. James's SAVE workshops are now always my first deliverables on the project plan."

— **Céiteach Mac Stiofan**, Digital Transformation Project Manager

"I love that the book references the frameworks but faces the reality that projects don't like to obey the rules of any specific framework so even the best PM is going to need to think on their feet."

— **Josh Pert**, CTO Virgin Experience Days

"While *Leading Impactful Teams* aims itself at project management, it's really focussed on people – how to work with, listen to, motivate and lead them and should be a must-read for anyone in a leadership position. The combination of the very frank, personable, open and honest writing and the fantastically clear illustrations really make the various concepts stick in your memory and make this a very easy but valuable read. James provides you with a smorgasbord of tools, techniques and concepts that are useful and relevant, regardless of what methodology you might be using, and I can see this become one of those well thumbed through books, covered in notes and Post-its that I will keep coming back to continuously for inspiration."

— **Stuart Halford**, Chief Information Officer at Goodbody

For Jessica, Sam and Thomas
— The greatest project of my life

Contents

Acknowledgements

It came as a bit of a surprise to me that I've written a book, and even more of a surprise that I had such a good time doing it. It started with the realisation, while working with Tais Krymova on pictures to explain project management concepts to stakeholders, that there was a better way to explain a lot of this stuff. Tais has been incredible to work with, turning my ideas into beautiful illustrations that get the points across in such an entertaining way. Despite the challenges she, and her friends and family are facing in Ukraine, she always produces amazing outcomes, and is a joy to work with.

I didn't really know where to start with structuring and editing a book, and Misha Gericke has emerged as my guide, mentor and champion throughout. Always challenging and coming up with ideas on how to express the concepts we have covered. Alongside her, Val Deacon has been a cheerleader of the first degree and helped me to navigate the confusing world of publishing.

The team at De Gruyter have been fantastic, since my very first conversation with Steve Hardman about working together. Jaya Dalal, Natalie Wills, Heather Goss and the rest of the team have been incredibly supportive in getting the book out there, in the best format and to as many people as possible.

Pau Matteo started as my virtual assistant and has become a friend, advisor, mentor and co-learner. Always positive, always hard-working, and never afraid to challenge me and help me shape the direction of the book and the business.

Many of the ideas and stories in this book were thrashed out on long walks in the Phoenix Park with my great friend Lewis Kelly. Thank you for the humour, support, and great banter, in good times and tough ones.

Over the years, I have been fortunate to be guided by many mentors who have each made invaluable contributions to the ideas, stories, and methodologies discussed in this book. I am profoundly grateful to each one of you. To Anna Bancroft, Pat Breslin, Clare Bradshaw, Gillian Brennan, Liezl Bruwer, Tom Brady, Barry Clark, Lorna Conn, Gary Clare, John Coolican, Jefferson Cowhig, Clare Filby, Leah Gainey, Stuart Houghton, Anne Heraty, Adam Kelly, Antony Keane, Michael Keegan, Creag Louttit, Helen Louttit, Niall McDevitt, Wendy McNulty, Cliona McCusker, Cormac Neill, Andrew O'Connor, Matthew Prebble, Cathal Quigley, and to countless others who have been a part of this journey with me, thank you.

My Mum and Dad are the most incredible parents. Such different personalities that have taught me so much. My Mum is kind-hearted, warm, supportive and trusting. My Dad has inspired me to be more and learn more every day. His ability to solve any problem and his work ethic are traits that I try to emulate every day. Between them they have taught me so much and I am eternally grateful.

https://doi.org/10.1515/9783111271149-202

Finally – to Eunice, the love of my life. There are no words to express how thankful I am to be able to spend every day with you. The best sounding board I could hope for, and the most fun person to be around. Supportive, kind, always keeping me motivated and driving me forward. For so many reasons you are everything.

Introduction – How Not to Do It

It started with a headache on a Monday afternoon.

As usual, I was extremely busy, juggling ten different things. I was trying to impress everyone and kept adding more and more responsibilities to my ever-growing list so that I could keep moving up the career ladder. Publicly, everything looked like it was going well. I'd been promoted to senior manager – a goal I had been aiming at for three years. My wife had recently given birth to our third child. I was taking on not only bigger projects but also more senior titles at work, and I had the trust and support of a wide circle of colleagues.

Privately, though, there were problems. I'd moved to a new country a few years ago and hadn't really built my own support network outside my wife's family and friends. We had three children aged under five, which is tough on anybody, and we were both working full-time. Looking back now, I realise that a lot of the pressure was psychological and derived from my own attitudes.

Since starting my career, I always had the attitude of doing 'whatever it takes' at work. Pretty much no matter what the opportunity or the request, I would always say yes to it. Working on the assumption that doing more work was the best way to have a successful career had gotten me this far and seemed to be paying off quite well. The problem was that, after my promotion, the amount of available work had ballooned beyond anything I had encountered before. I was running part of a large, technical regulatory project for a pillar bank in Ireland, with the biggest team I had ever managed. The project itself was stressful. It had aggressive deadlines that could not be moved, but very little clarity about what needed to be done and lots of moving parts across many IT systems. Our team also had to operate in a highly risk-averse environment that added bureaucracy to pretty much everything we were trying to do. Stakeholders with different views and different needs seemed to be everywhere, popping out of the woodwork every time you thought you nearly had something nailed down.

Alongside the project, my company had a culture of doing 'plus 1' activities. These were projects outside of our day job that added value to the company and could perhaps get you noticed at senior levels to help you get your next promotion. Sometimes, these were fun things like coordinating the company ski trip. Sometimes, they were more serious, like writing a white paper on the latest technological trends or running a community of practice. I had always done this kind of thing without any issues, but now I was a senior manager, and I had several of these activities on the go – most of them requiring an additional three or four hours a week on top of my extremely stressful project role.

https://doi.org/10.1515/9783111271149-204

One of the 'plus 1s' which I'd recently taken on was to become the client data protection lead for the account. This meant I was now responsible for making sure the hundreds of people working at this client for my consultancy were doing everything they should be doing around data protection. There was a training element to this, which I enjoyed, but the role also came with additional responsibility as I was the escalation point whenever an incident happened. The previous week, there had been a situation which had led to a couple of extremely late nights, and several new and highly stressed stakeholders.

Another 'plus 1' was as head of the analysis and design competency for the bank. While I wasn't particularly skilled in analysis or design, I was good at organising meetings and getting people to work together and learn from each other. This was a nice one as I was doing something I loved, but it came with a particular burden. I was responsible for a bureaucratic 'tick-box' exercise where I had to approve access requests for everybody in the group – about 400 people. Sure, how hard is it to approve an access request? That depends on how seriously you take it, and, like an idiot, I took it quite seriously. I was making phone calls to check everything was in order and then working through a time-consuming manual process for every request.

Unfortunately, it didn't stop with project work and 'plus 1s'. One of the members of my team in India was getting married and wanted to move to a different part of the country. He was a good guy who did great work on the project, and we had an office in the part of the country he wanted to move to. I took it upon myself to help him move rather than taking the easy option of simply 'rolling him off' the project. This meant I found myself embroiled in the bureaucracy of moving a colleague from one business entity to another from halfway around the world.

In short, the job was extremely busy. There were a few other things going on that piled on the pressure a bit more. My phone had broken, and people weren't able to get hold of me easily. My motorbike had started to become less reliable, and I just hadn't found time to get it fixed. This meant I had to build extra contingency into my commute to make sure that if the motorbike did break down, I would still have time for a mad dash to the office in a taxi to make my 8 a.m. daily meeting.

My wife, Eunice, was doing an amazing job of looking after our three young kids, but she was tired as well, and I was desperate to give her as many breaks as I could. I was responsible for the 'dream feed' for the baby at 11 p.m., and, as a rule, I tried to get up with the older two children if they needed something in the night, which was a regular enough occurrence. The levels of exhaustion we were both facing were nearing breaking point. Most parents have been there. This was our 'darkest hour'. It should all have gotten better soon as my wife was planning on going back to work in a couple of months, and we would be hiring a childminder.

We felt that adding another pair of (grown-up) hands into this mix would surely make all the difference.

Ahead of Eunice's return to work, we'd decided to teach Sam, our two-year-old, how to use the toilet. He'd reached the stage where he was able to realise that he needed to go, and you had about five seconds to react before an accident happened. On one memorable occasion, I left a full trolley of shopping in our local supermarket and sprinted across the car park, carrying him at arm's length (pointing forwards!) to the nearest toilet in a pub. We had made it just in time and saved the whole shopping trip from descending into an embarrassing, wet, smelly disaster. Let's just say I was starting to make some tactical mistakes due to not having enough time to make proper plans and think things through.

Anyway, after a few more mad dashes and lots of praise, we could see on the horizon a day when the number of nappy changes in the household would halve. Summer was coming and Thomas (the baby) might just start sleeping through the night. We'd be over the hump!

Then the toilet seat broke.

For a house where one of the children is potty training and there is a baby that needs supervising, the downstairs loo is a critical piece of infrastructure. Now, I've always prided myself on my ability to fix things around the house. You need a shelf put up? I'm your man. Building Ikea furniture – never happier. Painting a wall while listening to the cricket on the radio is my idea of heaven. But there are some jobs that are just awkward, difficult, and stressful to me. One of these is climbing around under sinks or behind toilets, undoing corroded nuts, and fiddling with pipes. I'm just not elegant or skilled in this situation. There is invariably a swear word and a skinned knuckle, and the job always takes at least three times as long as it should.

There was an innocuous text message on the phone from my wife: 'Please can you pick up a new toilet seat on your way home? The one in the downstairs toilet has broken.' I saw the message after my 10 a.m. meeting, and by 1 p.m. I had a tremendous headache.

I popped a couple of paracetamol and tried to get back to reviewing the requirements traceability matrix with the team, but something had changed for me that afternoon. I felt different. Not just stressed but overwhelmed. There were just too many things for me to do. And they were all important, all urgent.

Later that afternoon, I was in a meeting with a potential supplier of some software that could meet some of our requirements. It was a slow meeting and my boss texted me, 'I need to drop out for another meeting.' I texted him back, 'NP' to say that there was no problem. Unfortunately, my phone had autocorrected 'NP' to 'NO' and I'd hit send!

It was the kind of little mistake that I usually didn't make. I'd always check a text message before I hit send, especially one to my boss. A surge of adrenaline rushed through my body as I quickly texted, 'No Problem!' but he'd already seen my first response and given me a funny look. He slipped out of the meeting, and I got back to asking questions about the performance and security of the vendor's system. That night, I got home late and didn't fix the toilet seat.

The next day, the headache was still there and was absolutely throbbing. It was so bad that I decided I couldn't work. I told the team I wasn't well and locked myself in my bedroom, forcing myself to relax and try to get better. The whole day, all I could think about was the work piling up, the effort that my wife was putting in with the kids, and the guilt of not fixing the toilet seat, but I was completely incapacitated by the headache. I couldn't even open the curtains without causing a searing pain behind my eyes. As I lay there, everything running through my mind, exhausted, miserable, and in pain, I realised I needed to look after myself and change something.

By Wednesday, the headache had subsided a bit, so I got back onto the motorbike and went into the office for the 8 a.m. meeting. In the space of just one day out of the office, the issues had piled up on my desk: approvals, sign-offs, documents to review, plans to write, emails to respond to, and a presentation for a steering committee that was due next week, and I hadn't even started. I got my head down and started ploughing through the work. I was operating on pure adrenaline, at high speed, moving from task to task like a man possessed. That night, I got home from work by 6 and told Eunice how I was feeling. She was worried and suggested I go for a walk and get some fresh air.

I walked to the local park and found some long grass. This was 2016 and the concept of mindfulness was making its way into the corporate world, so I lay in the long grass, looking up at the blue sky above me and just trying to be 'in the moment'. The headache was still there, but it wasn't too bad. After half an hour or so, I went home. Eunice had called my parents and I spoke to them about how I was feeling. They were supportive but worried about me. They wanted me to get some help. I told them I'd see how if felt in the morning.

Thursday morning, I felt a lot better. Back into work, churning through emails, meetings, phone calls, bringing it all back on track, getting control of everything after my day off earlier in the week. I was solving problems, helping people, and feeling powerful and valuable like normal, but this time, there was a surreal haze over everything. It was like I was watching myself from the outside doing my work. On Friday morning, there was a monthly senior managers' meeting in a hotel on the other side of the city. I awoke at 5 a.m. with the headache pounding again. This was my chance to do something about the pressure. I wrote down notes about what was causing my stress, started to think about ways of explaining them to people, and prepared myself for a confrontation with my boss' boss, the managing director who headed up the account, about the level of pressure on everyone.

On the motorbike to the hotel, I was very calm. I arrived 45 minutes early for the 8 a.m. meeting and walked around the hotel gardens psyching myself up for the release that needed to come that morning. As I watched my colleagues arrive and get their coffees and pastries, I also saw my opportunity to speak to the MD. I went directly over to him, and very calmly, I said:

> 'I need to spend 20 minutes talking about my mental health in this meeting, and if you don't give me the floor, I will resign immediately and tell everyone that it's because you would not let me speak about my mental health.'

Both barrels – no holding back!

He was somewhat taken aback as we'd always had a good relationship, and this was completely out of the blue to him. He simply said, 'I trust you. The floor is yours.'

The 30 most senior people on the account, who were expecting a business update and a discussion on training plans, then received what can only be described as the presentation of my life. I explained about the stresses of the project, the plus 1s, the stakeholders, the bureaucracy, the sleepless nights, the Indian colleague who wanted to get married, the text message mistake, the dream feed, the potty training, the headaches, and finally, the toilet seat!

I'd done it. I'd shared my problems. It felt amazing!

It's still a bit hazy. I think there might have been some clapping. There was definitely some hugging and some tears. Everyone in that room felt some of the things that I was feeling, perhaps not to the same level, but I was right in the heart of it, and they all got it.

Immediately after that meeting, the pressure came off. Colleagues came up to me, asking how they could help. Senior people offered to find ways to reduce the amount of work. The corporate machine kicked in, and the indispensability of one person was proven, as it has been many times before, to be an illusion. One of the partners in the firm, Cliona, took me for a coffee and told to take some time off. She told me not to worry about anything, that they would support me. She also gave me the number of the Employee Assistance Programme set up specifically to help people with these kinds of problems. I left work at around 3 p.m. and sat with my wife in the kitchen that evening, planning exactly how we would relax over the next few days. We arranged for her sister to take the children and booked a hotel for the following night to get away, just the two of us.

Unfortunately, I still had the headache.

The next morning was Saturday. I woke up early again, this time with the baby. He and I played downstairs, but I could still feel this huge level of pressure bearing down on me. As soon as my wife woke up, I left the kids with her and went out for a walk. I called the Employee Assistance Programme number, but as it was 7:30 on a Saturday morning, they didn't have a specialist available to speak to me. They would call me back around 9 a.m.

Immediately after I put down the phone from that call, things started to get weird. I got an overwhelming feeling of not being in control of my actions and I started to become very worried about what I might do. I ran home and asked my wife to take the kids to her father's house around the corner so that I could 'relax' and wait for the EAP person to call me back. She was worried about me but got them out of the house. I tried to watch a couple of episodes of a comedy on the television to keep busy until I could speak to a specialist, but by 8:30 a.m., I was becoming quite manic about the state of my mental health. I ran over the road, banged on a neighbour's door, and blurted out that I was having a breakdown and I didn't know what to do.

I don't really remember much after that. I shouted a bit, locked myself out of the house, ran around, and generally behaved strangely – all the while holding on to one primeval thought: I am not in control, and I must not hurt anyone.

After what must have been about 15 minutes, an ambulance arrived, and professionals took over. I was rushed to the hospital with the ambulance sirens blaring, strapped to a trolley, and given some drugs to calm me down. My hands were strapped to my sides, I was unable to move, and for a couple of days I was isolated in a secure room with a series of large, strong-looking male attendants keeping watch over me. The experience of this "Psychotic episode" is still very vivid in my memory. I remember feeling completely out of control, unable to be sure what my next action would be, and extremely fearful that I would seriously hurt someone I cared about. The ambulance had been called in the nick of time, and in the end, everyone was fine, and it was just a bit of shouting and weird behaviour, but I still sometimes wonder what would have happened if the ambulance had not arrived when it did.

Eventually after several days of blood tests, spinal taps, and a good bit of medication to calm me down, the doctors diagnosed me with a very severe case of viral meningitis. The tissue around my brain had become infected and swollen. No wonder I'd had a headache for a week and had been feeling so much 'pressure'!

The diagnosis surprised me. I was absolutely convinced that I'd had a stress-related breakdown. To this day, I still feel very strongly that the whole episode was brought about by excessive stress from both external pressure and the pressure I was putting on myself. Whatever the cause, I knew things had to change.

When I reflected on these events a few months later, I realised that I had been trying for years to live up to my favourite poem by 'filling each unforgiving minute with sixty seconds' worth of distance run'. Being ambitious and pushing myself to achieve more were right at the heart of my self-image. I had believed that I could always work harder and make great things happen, but it turns out there is a level where that is simply not sustainable.

I realised that there was nobody else putting a limit on what I took on. I had several bosses, none of whom could have recognised just how much pressure I had put on myself, or how many different balls I was trying to juggle. The only person who could have realised it was me, and I was too damn busy to stand back and ask myself if what I was doing was sustainable. I'd heard the phrase 'work expands to fill the time available', but I was not putting limits on the time I was giving to work nor the amount I took on. As a capable project manager, I could always find things I could do to drive a project forwards. Every time I had a small amount of space to breathe, I squeezed something else into that gap until it just broke me.

Lying in the hospital bed that week, I got a video from my brother, who had recorded himself playing 'the Bare Necessities' on the guitar. One line struck me particularly strongly: 'The bees are buzzing in the tree to make some honey just for me'. There I was, being paid to lie in a bed while other people were picking up the slack back in the office. There was nothing I could or should do to help them and guess what – the work carried on! Sure, there was a bit of a bump as another project manager was assigned and picked up the project, and there were a couple of milestones missed. But nobody died, nobody got fired, everybody was OK. The real risk to life and limb had been from me putting far too much emphasis on my ability to fix everything, and it had caused this potentially fatal, and certainly terrifying, illness and incident. I resolved there and then to change my approach to work.

The bees are buzzing in the tree to make some honey just for me

Work does not simply expand to fill the time available. For ambitious, creative people, work is infinite! There is always something else that you could be doing to drive your goals forwards. If you don't have good structures and limits in place, you will fill up your working life with so many things that something will eventually break.

I wasn't allowed back into work for a couple of months after leaving the hospital and was strongly advised to go back slowly, so I was due to start with a three-day week. My wife was (understandably) very worried that I might get myself into a similar position again at some point in the future, so she came with me to meet Cliona before I returned to work.

On a sunny day, we sat outside a hotel near the office and talked about how I had ended up being so overwhelmed. We talked about the different roles I'd taken on, what was going on with my personal life, and how we might set things up for my future. Cliona reassured me that my experience was not something that anyone wanted to happen again, and that they would do whatever was necessary to support me in making the required changes.

We talked about what I most enjoyed about my job and what I was best at. I loved the aspects of my job around teaching, coaching, and helping others (I still do). One of my roles had been to lead the analysis and design competency on the account and help people be effective in those roles. We both agreed that I was much more suited to teaching and training project managers and, with a bit of shuffling around, we thought we might be able to create a full-time role where I could help other people become good at delivering projects.

The conversation then turned to something that Cliona and I both knew by the acronym DES – the Delivery Excellence School. DES was in a bad way and needed someone to take it on. It was a week-long training programme for people on the account to help them learn about project delivery. It was a fantastic idea and had been run twice, but both times, it had insufficient ownership. It had been cobbled together from other training courses and no one individual had an overall view of the programme, the flow of it, and the way the content tied together. DES needed someone to fix it and I was just the person.

So, it was settled. I would become the Project Management Competency Lead. I'd sort out DES and I would become responsible for ensuring that the 200 or so project managers were trained and supported to do a good job, all without being responsible for any of the actual projects! This was my dream job, and I loved it!

Over the next two years, I learnt everything I could about project management. I completed the PMP and Scaled Agile Framework certifications. I read everything I could find on the subject. I set up an internal podcast called 'The PM Competency Call' and I got to sit with experienced and less experienced project managers across the whole business, find out about their challenges, and help them figure out how to resolve them. I learnt about Design Thinking, Lean, Scrum, Kanban, and many other related fields and techniques, and I brought it all together into the Delivery Excellence School 2.0 to train others in this area.

DES 2.0 was so successful that even senior people on the account wanted to go on it, but many of them didn't have the time. So, we created 'Flex', a one-day training course on the key elements of delivering at the bank. Flex was tweaked for the different career levels and enabled us to train 120 people on the core elements in just one week. By this stage, the PM competency had grown so successful that I had a small team behind me, and I had taken over responsibility for pretty much all the training on the account while continuing to coach and guide my colleagues as individuals and teams.

In November 2018, while teaching another round of Delivery Excellence School, I received a call from a head-hunter on behalf of the largest recruitment company in Ireland. They had heard about what I was doing, and they wanted me to apply for a role as Chief Information Officer and sort out some significant problems in their IT department. After going through the process, I was offered the job. However much I loved what I was already doing, I couldn't say no to my first chance at a 'C-level' role at a major PLC and one of the most recognisable companies in Ireland.

I joined Cpl in February 2019, and over the next three and a half years, I trained the team and the company in project delivery. It was refreshing to have the decision-making power and I was given full responsibility by the CEO and CFO to make IT really work for the company. We went from having many production issues with legacy applications and failing to deliver very much for the business to winning awards for our technology and developing a fantastic reputation within the organisation for completing what they needed when they needed it. The tips, techniques, and approaches we used make up most of this book, and I hope that you will enjoy using them as much as we did.

Many people get themselves into stressful and difficult positions. I now firmly believe that it is up to project managers to look after themselves and their teams. It is our responsibility to make sure that the work we are doing is sustainable, enjoyable, and valuable, and that with a diverse toolbox of techniques, many more projects can be delivered more effectively – without any of us needing to end up in hospital.

The content of this book is now used to train aspiring and experienced project managers in what I consider to be the very best techniques, approaches, and ideas available today. People have described that training as game changing, completely revolutionizing the way they think about their projects, their teams, and themselves.

With Tais' illustrations to help, I hope you will find the following pages valuable, memorable, and immediately applicable to whatever projects you are working on. Whether it's a different way of thinking about how you use contingency to drive much more valuable conversations or simply structuring your meetings better to give your team a chance to add their input more effectively, I hope that you will benefit from the years of learning, failure, success, and refinement that have gone into this book and the training course it supports.

Enjoy!

Chapter 1
Project Management is Broken

Many teams are drowning in work that comes at them from all directions

We all manage projects. Whether it is organising a family holiday, renovating our house, or running a project at work, we find ourselves responsible for making all the things that need to happen, happen. Unfortunately, only a very small number of us ever get the opportunity to be trained in project management, and even that training can be quite academic and difficult to apply to the real world. This book is about making project management simple and giving you the skills, tips, and techniques that you can use to make all your projects successful.

I have managed many projects and have spent the last few years teaching project management to seasoned project professionals, colleagues who need to run a project alongside their day job, and students just starting out in their careers. I've found it is quite rare for people to take a step back and think about how they are going to manage their project. When they do take that time, and if they have the right support in place, I've seen people find many ways of reducing the amount of effort required, working more effectively with colleagues, and improving their

https://doi.org/10.1515/9783111271149-001

projects' outcomes. With relatively few nudges in the right direction, you are more likely to succeed in your goals, reduce your stress levels, improve your relationships, and hopefully even have some fun in your project.

While I started my career as a project manager running traditional 'waterfall' projects (more on that later), I have become convinced that there is no single way to run a successful project. Instead, I prefer to think about project management as a series of lenses, techniques, and tips that can be used to get to a desired outcome. The best project managers will be aware of many of these tools and spend time each day to pick and choose the right ones to use based on the situation that is in front of them.

Project management requires experience, negotiation, empathy, drive, vision, organisation, and a constantly growing toolbox of techniques and skills. Nobody walks out of a college course or university degree in project management ready to manage a project, and no employer in their right mind will hand over important projects to someone with no experience.

This means that most project managers start out as something else. I was a developer and business analyst before I knew enough to even start thinking about becoming a project manager. Many people fall into project management after simply being asked to take on a project because they know a lot about the area that is being affected by the project. Others grow from being a specialist in one skill set to being asked to take on more, and many people are just the last person standing when all the others have been ruled out.

Projects are often so urgent and important that the opportunity to learn on them is very limited. The people asked to manage these projects are instantly in the fire, expected to push things forwards. They need to manage a team and stakeholders who range from experienced professionals to brand-new joiners. They are required to negotiate a complex environment full of pitfalls, nuance, and politics that only become apparent to people after they have been in a company for several years.

By the time they realise they are a project manager, people are often overwhelmed with the many hats they need to wear and tasks they need to do. Unfortunately, most find that stopping to learn how to become a project manager is simply not an option because they are just too busy!

When I stand in front of a room full of people who have signed up for an 'Introduction to Project Management' training course, they are generally an extremely diverse bunch of people, with an enormous variation in experience and skills. The one thing they have in common is that they are facing an exceptionally complex challenge, one that they have not been prepared for.

Project Management Frameworks

So what training has traditionally been on offer to these new project managers? Keen, motivated, and ready to take on their first challenge – exam-based certification.

Learning for certification is not the whole story of becoming a successful project manager. In some ways it is very useful. When I completed my PMP (Project Management Professional) certification, I knew all the language of project management, and I knew that I had learned all the things that I "should" know to manage a project. But I still felt that there was a gap in my knowledge and a huge gap in skills.

Passing an exam like PMP is a strong signal that you are taking project management seriously, and that you are prepared to learn about it. It also tells potential employers that you are good at studying and can pass exams. These are all OK things, but they do not tell anyone how you will treat your team, or how well you will prioritise work, or what kinds of decisions will be made on your projects.

Project management frameworks have been discussed and debated in meetings and committees and deliberately made generic so that they can be applicable to every organisation and project.

Alec Issigonis, the designer of the Mini, once described a camel as a horse designed by a committee. The problem with the project management frameworks out there is that they are also designed by committees. They are designed to be applicable to all projects, and following them blindly without adapting them for your company or project can lead to a lot of unnecessary work, and missing out on some great opportunities to make good decisions.

PM frameworks – the horse designed by a committee

I see project management skills as a set of lenses, techniques, and tips that can be applied to different projects. Not all will be applicable all the time, and an impactful project manager will pick the right tools and techniques to use given the organisation they are working in, the project they are working on, and the team and stakeholders they are working with.

The framework that you use, whether it's PMI, PRINCE2, Scrum, SAFE, LeSS, or any of the others, will give you some structure, but it's the project manager's skills and behaviours that really count. I'd recommend that project managers learn and understand some of these frameworks at a high level, but you should look at them as part of your toolbox rather than a hard-and-fast recipe for project success. Just because PRINCE2 suggests that you use stage gates does not mean that your project or organisation needs stage gates all the way through the project. Just because Scrum uses daily stand-ups does not mean that they are required for your project. You should be aware of both stage gates and daily stand-ups and use neither, either, or both on your project, depending on the circumstances you are facing.

In many ways, project management would benefit from an apprentice structure like those that have been used for centuries to teach other skilled practitioners like plumbers or doctors. Unfortunately, very few companies are prepared to put two project managers on a project so that the junior PM can learn from the senior one. This means that PMs very often spend their time doing things that are not commensurate with their skill set. Experienced senior PMs spend a lot of time filling in the documentation that is required by their organisation, and junior PMs are often out of their depth, trying to manage complex stakeholder and team relationships that require nuance and experience.

While I think it's unlikely that we'll change this culture of expecting PMs to wear all the different hats regardless of the stage of their career, perhaps we might get a few people to think about how to delegate or escalate tasks to colleagues with the right level of experience and reduce the overall levels of stress and frustration that PMs go through.

What Makes an Impactful Project Manager?

If you turn up to work as a project manager and just go through the motions, or follow someone else's framework without understanding it, you will not be as effective as you could be. In fact, it's much worse than that. Because of the time pressures, expectations, and urgency that surround so many projects, bad project management reduces the team's output and gets in the way of delivering value to the organisation.

A great project manager can deliver a better outcome, faster and with less cost, using the same team as an average or a bad project manager. In many cases, things that look like problems with the project itself could have been avoided if the project manager had more experience, better support, or better training. I have proven time and again that, with the right training, guidance, and support, most people can significantly increase their impact as a project manager. For business leaders, there are very few opportunities that will provide a higher return on investment than in helping your project managers to become more impactful. To illustrate the point, I'll give you an example.

My team was once asked by a senior person in the business to build a new system where hiring managers could expose their diaries through the website to allow interviewees to book an interview. The team started working on the solution, and within a couple of weeks, they had identified a few ways that this could be done. All the ideas were technically sound and could be done in three to six months. The business case for the project was good, and we had approval to invest around €100,000 to build the system. When the team presented the options to me, I could have simply said, 'great – let's build it,' and off we went.

I didn't do that.

Instead, I talked to a few other stakeholders in the company and shared the idea. I wanted to build a coalition of other parts of the business where something like this could be useful. Within a few days, we had several more departments interested in the functionality, and the business case was at least triple the size of the original target group. Then I set up a discussion with a couple of technical stakeholders from outside the project team to get their ideas. One of those guys was keeping up to speed with Microsoft's releases and mentioned that they had just released a 'bookings' function in the system that we already had. We checked it out, did some tests, ran a quick pilot, and, within three weeks, we had rolled out the new booking functionality to a large business unit that was delighted with the outcome. This required no development, only a little bit of configuration and testing. The total cost of the project was less than €8,000.

If we hadn't engaged the other stakeholders – both technical and business – we would have spent 10 times as much and worked really hard to create functionality that we already had in our estate for free. Worse, we would only have offered it to a small part of our business.

The impact of that project could have been 10 times less value for 10 times more effort. Making good decisions with the right stakeholders pays enormous dividends!

The rest of the book will give you lots of tips and techniques on how to become an impactful project manager, but it is worth spending a few minutes just thinking about the general themes that will make you more effective. Like many people, I tend to understand images faster than text, so throughout the book, we have included memorable images that will help you to remember these tips. To help with this, we have created two characters, Jill and John.

Jill

Jill is an impactful project manager. She is constantly looking for ways to add value to her projects and minimise the effort that needs to be put in. She trusts her team and gives them the freedom and support they need to solve problems and take advantage of opportunities themselves. Jill is not particularly organised naturally, so she uses structures and processes to make sure that the important things get done and done well. She works very hard on her people skills, always trying to see the situation from the other person's point of view and make sure that everyone's views, ideas, and concerns are included in the discussion and taken seriously.

Jill knows that a project's success or failure is entirely down to her, and she takes extreme ownership of everything that is going on. However, rather than working harder and harder and micro-managing all the tasks, she focuses her efforts on prioritisation, transparency, escalation, delegation, and communication. She makes sure that she is using the resources available to her in the most valuable way. She is optimistic, proactive, creative, trusting, and confident. She believes that if you give people the right tools, support, and guidance, they can do amazing things. She also takes full responsibility for all the mistakes and mishaps on the project while also giving credit and praise freely and thoroughly when things go well.

Jill encourages the team to learn all the time. She creates opportunities for them to teach and coach each other and she leads by example. She's constantly growing her own skills and capabilities, and then shares those learnings with others. She gives everyone the benefit of the doubt, always assuming that they are doing their best and have the project's interests at heart, even if they disagree with what she or others are saying. This culture permeates the team, and everyone leans on each other's strengths and helps with each other's weaknesses.

Jill cares passionately about the project's outcomes for the organisation, her team members, and her stakeholders and wants to make sure that everyone has the right level of balance in their work and personal life.

This is Jill and her team:

Jill – an impactful project manager

John

John is a very different type of project manager. He has worked very hard to get where he is and is proud of the senior position he holds. He has lots of strong opinions and is not afraid to share them. He gets frustrated with people who disagree with him or make mistakes and believes that time spent on experiments and learning should not be covered by the project. He likes to see the outputs of everyone's work – making sure they are working hard all the time, whether it is on something valuable or not. John doesn't mind asking people to work late or cancel holidays – he's had to do it throughout his career, so why shouldn't they?

John keeps everything in his head. He's clever, and as long as **he** knows what's going on, then everything is OK. He shares information when necessary but does not like people to see details because he believes they will hold him to unreasonable expectations or timelines. He builds extra contingency into his estimates so that he can deal with issues when they arise, but he does not spend a lot of time managing risks because they might never become an issue.

John has been successful in his career so far, and the ways he works have stood the test of time, so why should they change? He values knowledge and experience over a positive attitude and the desire to learn and doesn't really trust people until he has worked with them for at least two years.

This is John and his team:

John – a traditional project manager

Project Management Training Is Changing Too

A lot of project management training has been left behind by the advances in the industry over the last few years. For a professional, well-paid career employing millions of hard-working, intelligent people around the world, some of the available training is awful. It is either given too early (at university) and built on academic theory or is so aligned to teaching a set of standards provided by a certification body that it is more like memorising a set of terminology than learning a craft. When I did my PMP certification, I had to re-learn everything I knew about project management to fit within that organisation's framework and terminology. I was motivated to do it because it was something I had agreed with my boss to do at the time, and it would enable me to be charged out at a higher rate to our clients – and therefore could be a good part of the company's rationale for promoting me.

While I was learning about it, there was very little focus on the practicalities of how I could use the framework on my projects. I walked away feeling that, if I did all the things it was suggesting, I would create a lot of admin work for myself and not get a lot of benefit for the project in return.

Since PMP and PRINCE2 were first developed, there have been huge advances in our understanding of human behaviour and amazing developments in the tools and technologies available to project managers. Whereas once everyone worked in the same office, teams are now often spread all over the world, and a lot of successful teams never meet each other face to face. The Agile Movement has popularised frameworks like Scrum and Kanban, which allow people to be highly effective, with a much-reduced requirement for documentation and bureaucracy. However, these approaches are designed for software delivery. They do not take into account the organisation around the delivery team, the need for risk management, rollout plans, and dealing with a complex stakeholder environment.

Project management tools like Jira, Monday.com, and Trello have made managing teams and tasks much easier. Behavioural economics has taught us to deal with other people in the ways that they actually behave, rather than through some idealised unrealistic expectation that they will never make a mistake and will always do what they promise.

The Project Management Institute (PMI), who developed the PMP certification, have recognized this shift in the approach to project management and are at the forefront of this movement to build better skills for Project Managers. They have introduced the concept of "Power Skills" in recent years to support this need for practical, human approaches to delivering projects. This is a very positive move and is helping to shift the emphasis in the industry from seeing project management as a set of technical skills and approaches to seeing it as a human-centred craft that guides rather than dictating and takes account of the differences between people and organisations.

The ideas and approaches in this book and in the accompanying training courses are designed to give practical advice to help people to implement these power skills. After reading this book, I hope that you'll not only understand why they are important but you'll also have dozens of ideas on how to demonstrate these skills.

I believe all this new knowledge and better understanding should be taught to project managers. It will give them the confidence, strength of relationships, and support around them to always do what is right for the organisation, especially when circumstances on the project change. That's so much better than expecting them to mindlessly follow a plan because that is what was decided in a meeting months ago.

Why Does This Matter?

The focus in many organisations on outdated ways of doing things and expectation of perfectly rigid and rational behaviour means that projects are very often run much less effectively than they could be. People work diligently on the wrong tasks. They produce mountains of paperwork for very little business benefit. They treat each other as obstacles to get around rather than collaborators to work with and learn from. Plans are followed because they are 'the plan' rather than because they are the right thing to do. People spend a lot of time fighting fires and dealing with "busy work" rather than giving themselves time to think and make sure they are being effective. They switch tasks frequently and deal with constant interruptions, which sap their energy and impede their ability to concentrate.

Many projects also end up in a 'mad dash' to meet deadlines or commitments that are made. Rather than having a tough conversation and making joint decisions with stakeholders in a high-trust, transparent environment. People put pressure on each other, which very often leads to long hours, weekend work, and cancelled holidays. As soon as one project hobbles over the line, the next one starts up, and that high-pressure environment builds up again. The result? People end up getting disillusioned with the work, burn out, and leave the company.

What Can We Do About It?

In this age of human-centric, enlightened management, the old excuses of having to meet deadlines or 'doing what it takes' to get things over the line are no longer acceptable. People burning out or working long hours for weeks on end are an indication of poor training and a lack of appreciation of the compromises required in balancing resources. Project managers have a responsibility to make work sustainable and enjoyable for everyone involved. We have great power to affect the well-being of our colleagues, and it is our responsibility to do everything we can to help our teams thrive and be successful. Using the lenses, tips, and techniques in this book and the accompanying training, I know from personal experience and the experiences of the many project managers that I've trained that you can look forward to a much more successful career, better relationships with your colleagues, and projects that are so fulfilling, enjoyable, and impactful that you'll want to tell your friends and family all about them.

As you go through this book, I recommend that you keep your current and past projects in mind. Keep asking yourself the question, 'should I be doing something differently?' Most importantly, if the answer is yes, take action right now. When you see an idea you like, put the book down for a couple of minutes and set up that workshop, take a note of what to talk about in your next meeting, or think about how you are going to change one of your interactions with a colleague. By the end of the final chapter, I promise that you'll have many new approaches, new ideas, and great techniques to help you become an impactful project manager.

Chapter 2
The Lenses – How to Think About Your Project Like an Expert

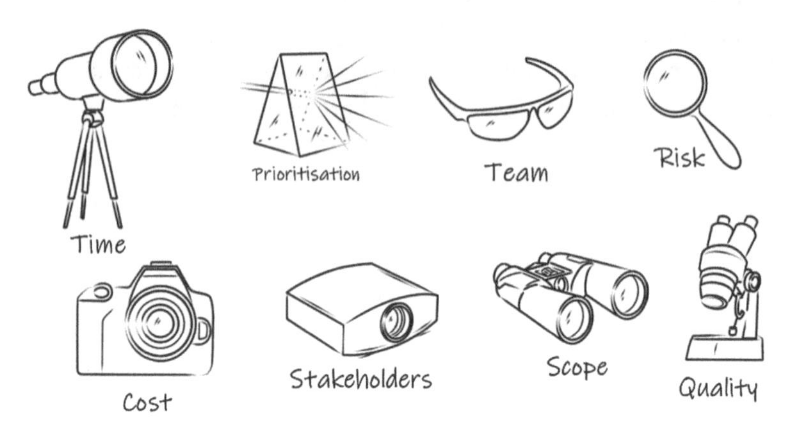

The lenses of project management

Experienced project managers have a kind of 'sixth sense' for spotting trouble on projects. They seem to know where to spend their time to keep the project on track or to avoid potential pitfalls. My father has a saying that he uses every time my siblings or I have a setback: 'Experience is worth what it cost you.' He's right – getting experience can be painful, but having it is extremely valuable.

I would also argue that experience isn't the only way to learn. Most of the tips and techniques I have used over my career were developed through other people's experience. While it is possible that I was the first person to teach agile methodologies using a marble run and growth mindset using balloon animals, I certainly didn't invent affinity clustering or the daily stand-up. I copied other people's approaches and ideas and made these tools my own.

I asked myself how I (and other experienced project managers) think about our projects and what this 'sixth sense' really is. I believe that by looking at your project through different lenses, you can imitate all those years of experience and cover pretty much all the bases on your project.

One of the biggest constraints and the biggest asset any project manager has is their own time. You need to decide how you spend that time to best benefit your project's goals. If you have a very experienced team, with highly motivated colleagues who really know what they are doing, you might spend most of your time out in the rest of the organisation, nurturing relationships and communicating progress to key stakeholders. If you have a new team, you might need to spend a

https://doi.org/10.1515/9783111271149-002

lot more time on coaching, training, and hiring. A difficult working environment might mean that you need to spend a lot of time improving conditions so your colleagues can get on with the project work. You might be operating in a heavily regulated or constrained environment, which requires you to spend a lot of time applying for budget, taking the project through stage gates, and ensuring that everything is in place for the auditors at the end.

Whatever your environment and project, there are eight key lenses that you should regularly check in on to make sure that you are not missing any angles on your project. Some will take more time and effort than others, depending on your circumstances, but they are all worth standing back and considering in terms of how they affect your project and how you are managing them. These lenses will form the structure of this book and, as you practice looking at your projects through them, your instincts will become more attuned to when one of them needs a bit more attention.

Some projects require more focus on risk than others. Some projects are heavily constrained by cost or time, and others have an overriding requirement for very high quality. Whatever type of project you will be running, it's important to ramp your level of focus on each of these lenses up and down in response to your circumstances to make sure you are doing the right things at the right times. For ease of reference, the eight lenses are:

- Scope
- Prioritisation
- Time
- Cost
- Quality
- Risks (and Assumptions, Dependencies, and Issues)
- Team
- Stakeholders

I chose the analogy of lenses because it gives you a sense of what it feels like to look at your project through each of these themes.
All of these lenses will be explained in greater detail later in the book, with examples, techniques, and tips that will help you manage them. For now, it's useful just to get a feel for each of them with a brief introduction.

Scope

This is the 'what' of the project and it must be fundamentally underpinned by the 'why'. Many projects are unclear on what is in scope, what is out of scope, and, even worse, why those things have been included or excluded. Clarity over project scope and prioritisation of the most valuable outcomes are crucial to project success. Many projects spend huge amounts of money, time, and resources on things that are not valuable to the projects' outcomes. We will spend time going into how to manage scope, but the biggest takeaway will be that you can't do everything, so do the most valuable and easiest things.

I have used the image of a sculpture to represent scope. Like an abstract sculptor who has an idea of what they want to achieve, but is guided by the material they are working with, impactful project managers will shape the scope of the project over time as they understand more of the constraints and opportunities they are working with. What you end up with may not be exactly what people thought it would be when they started.

Prioritisation

This is probably the lens that people miss most often and, by missing it, causes a lot of waste in projects. It is so easy to do the wrong things through inertia, avoiding the difficult conversation, or simply not thinking about project priorities often enough. Prioritisation is not well covered by most of the existing books and training on project management, and yet it is the single most important skill for all of us. Deciding how and where we spend our time and resources is critical to success in projects and life. If you are not actively prioritising your efforts, you are at the whim of other people's agendas.

The rest of the headings on this list will be familiar to people who have been trained as project managers, but prioritisation is different. I have spent a lot of time in this book helping you to figure out prioritisation, and if you master this skill, you really will become an impactful project manager.

I have used the sieve to represent prioritisation, because project managers should actively and intentionally decide what is included and what is not.

Time

When people think about a project plan, they very often think about the project's timeline. How long will it take? What will be done first? What are the dependencies on other things that need to happen? If you are managing a high-profile project, the timeline can become the most important element that will be discussed by stakeholders. For projects that are not going well, the place where that becomes most obvious is when milestones or deadlines start to be missed.

The secret here is that you do not have a crystal ball, so you need to manage people's expectations and make sure that you have great communication about the other aspects of the project. Doing this is crucial to ensuring that people are happy with whatever timeline the project ends up hitting, because they made the decisions that drove and impacted the timeline.

The crystal ball image represents time because it is critically important that you do not pretend to be able to see the future. Any predictions about what will happen should be treated as just that - predictions - and given an appropriate level of confidence in your discussions. Some predictions are very likely to come true but others are much more uncertain and you need to communicate that uncertainty as well as the prediction itself.

Cost

Along with timeframe, cost is the most visible element of your project, and the one that the most senior people will be interested in. The costs can be explicit (materials, contractors, rent, etc.) or implicit (the hidden costs of the organisation that do not appear on an invoice – the team's time or the efforts of other parts of the organisation and management). As with time, the key here is to make sure that whatever the costs end up being, the right people feel that they have control over them, and that they are actively involved in the decisions that drive or save costs.

I have used the image of the wallet with a belt around it to represent cost because budget can be hard to unlock, and spending must be treated with thought and intentionality.

Quality

Quality is one of the least used but most powerful levers that project managers have. If you ask any stakeholder how many defects they want in the product, they will all say 'none'. Unfortunately, there has never been a project that didn't have any defects. There are some projects where all the defects got fixed, but these tend to be in highly risk-averse environments like space travel and medical devices where the cost and timeline are secondary to the life-and-death consequences of quality issues. Unless you are working in these kinds of environments, you will simply not have the budget or the time to be perfect, so the question will become, 'how good does it need to be?'

The other thing to bear in mind is that there are diminishing returns to effort when it comes to quality. You can get something 80% right with relatively little effort, but taking it to 90% perfect might cost twice as much and 95% might cost twice as much again. By the time you get to 99% or 99.9%, you are often spending huge effort and resources to check absolutely everything in the hope that you might find any remaining issues. Again, the key here is around communication. If you can manage your stakeholders such that they expect to have a few defects, you can make the difficult discussions late in the project much easier and hopefully keep everyone happy.

I have kept with the lenses theme here, using the microscope because quality is about providing the right level of scrutiny on the outputs of your project. Think about zooming in and out based on the risk appetite of your organisation to focus in on the appropriate level of testing.

Risks (and Assumptions, Dependencies, and Issues)

Risk management is heavily ingrained in some organisations and completely lacking in others. I worked in financial services for several years after the financial crisis and the culture of risk management led to some extremely conservative decisions being made. Managing your risks appropriately is part of the art of project management. Too much risk management and you are wasting a lot of effort on things that probably won't happen and wouldn't matter that much if they did. Too little and you will find yourself in constant firefighting mode as issues that could have been avoided repeatedly hit the project.

Risks are related to assumptions, dependencies, and issues, and there is a life cycle to these that we'll explain more later in the book. For now, it is worth remembering that it is much easier and more effective to manage risks and dependencies using assumptions and contingency than it is to manage issues because you were not proactive enough. Trust me. When you've been through really serious issue management, you will see the value of managing risks before they hurt you.
The analogy with the shark in the water is clear here for risks. The goal is to be aware of it, treat it with respect, and make sure it doesn't become an issue!

Team

Nothing gets done in a project without the team who will do the work. Managing, motivating, training, hiring, and supporting your team is critical to the success of any project. One of the biggest pitfalls that some project managers fall into is failing to fight for the right team or not being creative enough to match the team you can create with the scope that is committed to. Training, negotiation, and prioritisation are often required to make sure that the resources you have are maximised, and that the project's scope aligns with the team that are available to deliver it.
I used the idea of a band here to show that everybody is different, and many of the people on your team will be able to do stuff that you can't do. The skill is in putting the right people in the right places and giving them the right tools, training and support to make music together as a group.

Stakeholders

A recurring theme across all the other lenses through which a project manager works is that you will need to work with other people. If you can set people's expectations well, give them control over the decisions they care about, use resources they are willing to provide, and not give them any nasty surprises, there is a good chance that whatever the project's outcome, they will still consider you to be a good project manager. How you manage your stakeholders will go a very long way to the project's success and its reputation. If you can make sure that you and your team have a great reputation, many of the other elements of managing the project become much easier.

So, what is a reputation? It's how other people perceive you. It doesn't matter how good a job you are doing if everyone thinks you are doing a bad job, so while it might seem a little Machiavellian, showing your project in its best light is something you really need to spend time and effort on. Different stakeholders will need to be engaged in different ways, which takes a lot of effort, but there is very little that is more valuable for a project manager to do than ensuring that all project stakeholders are getting what they need.

The watercooler image here is to remind us that managing stakeholders is nuanced and human. Different people need different levels and types of communication at different times.

Once you have these lenses in your mind, it's a good idea to keep that list somewhere handy and check in with it a couple of times a week. When you are writing your status report, updating the steering committee, or planning a workshop with the team, it's useful to just cast your eye over the project management lenses and check whether there is an angle you are missing on a particular piece of work. As you use the lenses every day, you will build that project manager's 'sixth sense' that automatically checks against the list. A new issue will come up, and you'll immediately think, 'There's a stakeholder impact here. I better get some comms out.' Or you'll be sitting in a prioritisation session and a new piece of functionality will be discussed, and you'll think, 'Hang on a second! I can smell a risk. Better dig into this a bit more.' It's this 'sixth sense' that distinguishes the great PMs from those who are just ticking the boxes. While it's taken me 20 years to build up this experience and hone it to a level where it's really ingrained, you can get a lot of the benefit just by having this list of lenses on a Post-it note on your desk.

So, with this new superpower of being able to look at your project from all the right angles, the next thing you'll need are some tools to help solve the myriad problems and opportunities that you will come across.

Chapter 3
Techniques and Tips – It's Easy If You Know How!

To successfully navigate a complicated landscape
you need a toolbox of skills and techniques

Along with the sixth sense of looking through lenses at your project, you will also need some skills to be a successful project manager. There are very few professions where you'll have to be as versatile as in project management. You'll need to switch easily from a detailed conversation about the minutiae of the project through to negotiating with an angry stakeholder or stepping back and figuring out a complex technical problem with many moving parts. The best project managers know when to push hard and when to take input. They can spot where there is a problem on their team and jump in with some coaching while making sure their priorities are the ones being worked on. It is a serious balancing act, and many project managers would say it's not only a different challenge every day, but often a different challenge every hour.

That is a huge part of what makes project management such a rewarding career. No two days are ever the same. There is a constant opportunity to learn new things about your team members, stakeholders, and yourself. There are also no 'right' answers because whatever the decision or approach you choose, the alternative will not happen, so you'll never know if it would have been better.

A project manager's skills are many and varied, and we'll talk about them a lot in this book. Fundamentally, though, it's all about the people. Where possible, project managers shouldn't be doing the work of the project, making decisions, or even generating ideas. It's how you work with and manage the people in and

https://doi.org/10.1515/9783111271149-003

around your project that will determine the success or failure of what you are trying to achieve.

I was lucky enough to have a very long motorbike ride to and from work early in my career. At the time, there weren't streaming services or podcasts, and I wanted to use the time effectively, so I added the audio version of Dale Carnegie's *'How to Win Friends and Influence People'* to my iPod. As I was riding the motorbike with no free hands, and I had the playlist on repeat, I found that when I finished the book, it just restarted, and I began listening to the whole book again. When I got to work, I got on with my day and never got round to uploading another book to listen to. In this way, I must have listened to that audiobook 10 or 20 times over the course of a few months.

Every time I'd get to work, I'd be in a different section of the book and would have that part fresh in my mind ready to use. Each day, new problems would be presented to me, and each day, I'd have a fresh tool right at the front of my mind ready to use with my colleagues. Whether it was making sure that I didn't criticise, or admitting when I was wrong confidently and proactively. I followed Carnegie's principles and honed and practiced my skills in winning friends and influencing people. And it worked! Like magic, I found that, where I might have struggled to change someone's mind one week, I was able to resolve some of the thorniest conflicts I'd come across the next week, just by finding out a bit more about their point of view, respecting their opinions, and letting them do most of the talking.

Many of Carnegie's approaches and ideas form the foundation of the skill tips in this book – hopefully with the additional context of 20 years of project management experience to give them even more insight. My favourite piece of advice – the most powerful one of all of them – is to try every day, and in every interaction, to see things from the other person's point of view. When you build this principle into your mindset, and really try to live by it, you find that the world opens up in a very different way. If your first port of call for every discussion is to find out what other people think and to take it into genuine consideration, you'll find there is huge value in every single one of those other people's opinions. Whether it's a risk that you haven't thought of or a constraint on resources that you weren't aware of, the reasons why people disagree with you are amongst the most important things for a project manager to take into consideration. As Carnegie puts it:[1]

> *'If out of reading this book you get just one thing—an increased tendency to think always in terms of other people's point of view and see things from their angle—if you get that one thing out of this book, it may easily prove to be one of the building blocks of your career.'*

I have to say, I couldn't agree more!

---

1 Carnegie, D. (2006). *How to Win Friends and Influence People.* Vermilion (p. 46).

It's a common occurrence for a project manager to have identified something that needs to be done, but not to know enough detail to write the plan or to figure out the costs or even work out which tasks are needed next. Many project managers will fall back on their own experience and just start figuring out the answers. If you are highly knowledgeable about the area you are working in and you have a full understanding of what's needed, there is a chance that this approach will get you started on your project in a way that feels like progress and has a reasonable chance of success.

This is what I call the 'subject matter expert' (SME) approach to project management, and it's often where people start on their project management careers. You have been working in a role for a few years and you are familiar with the context and the processes. You have good relationships and people respect your opinions. Then one day, your boss comes to you and asks you to take on a new project. It makes sense because you know a lot about the subject and could probably do a lot of the work yourself.

This first project is going to be about cutting your teeth and you have all the advantages, so there is a good chance for success. Unfortunately, there is also a big risk. The most likely outcome in this scenario is that because you are both a subject matter expert and the project manager, you can do a lot of the work yourself and, unfortunately, a lot of people will know this! I have often seen SME project managers become the most stressed and overworked people on the project.

Finding the balance between doing the project work and the many responsibilities of a project manager is almost – if not completely – impossible. Depending on your natural inclination, you will either roll up your sleeves and focus on the work and forget about the really important project management activities; or you will diligently update your stakeholders and run your status meetings, but find that the tasks allocated to you are falling behind or (worse!) being done in the evenings and over the weekend, when you should be spending time doing whatever else you enjoy doing.

The SME project manager is very often a stressful and exhausting role to take on. If you find yourself in this position, you really have only three options:

1. Be the project manager, but refuse to do any of the project tasks.
2. Be the SME, but don't take on responsibility for the overall delivery of the project.
3. Try to do everything.

I would recommend that you only go for number 3 on very small projects where you are highly confident of being able to deliver. If not, it's time for a 'difficult conversation' with someone to make sure that you take on only one role on the project. We'll cover difficult conversations later in the book, but suffice it to say, your life will be much easier if you are prepared for and take on difficult conversations and handle them well.

Whichever of these three roles you end up in on the project, I have good news! There are some superb tools and techniques that you can use to make sure that you are making good decisions, getting the help and support you need, and really making progress on your project goals. These tools will be spread out throughout this book in the places where they align to a particular area. However, I want to be clear that there is no one situation where each tool is the only option, and no tool that can only be used in one situation. The skill and experience of the impactful project manager is to understand and practice these tools and techniques and treat them like a toolbox to dip into at the appropriate times.

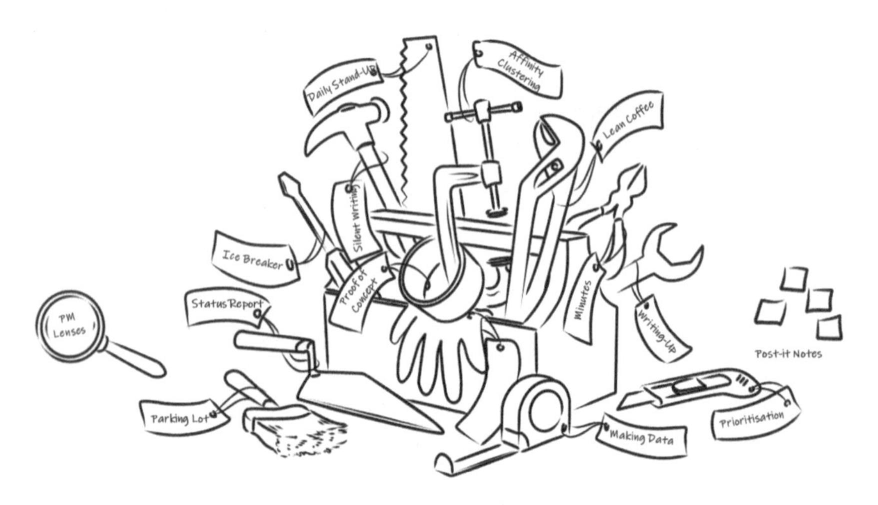

The project manager's toolbox

In the same way that a hammer and nails can be good for attaching two pieces of wood and a screwdriver and screws can do the same job, it will be your familiarity with these tools that will help you decide when to use each one. Your experience will help you to become more skilled at picking and using them over time.

There are many skills dotted throughout this book. They are very often just good management skills, but we're applying them specifically to projects here. Before we get into the detailed discussion on each of the lenses, there are a few general techniques that are going to be useful in many different scenarios.

Caves, Commons, Collaboration, and Contemplation

Before you do anything on a project, it is worth thinking about the work environment. It's important that the environment you choose to work in suits the work that is being done. Since the pandemic in 2020, work environments have changed a lot and work practices have become much more flexible. This is great because it allows you to change the environment for your team depending on the work that is being done at the time. I like to think about the environments in four broad groups: commons, caves, collaboration, and contemplation.

Commons and caves

Commons is your traditional office environment. Probably an open office space where people can see each other, overhear what's going on, build relationships, grab a coffee, and generally keep the buzz and fun of the office alive. This is a great general workspace, good for helping more junior members of the team learn from their colleagues, and quite efficient in terms of keeping everyone informed with what is going on. Depending on the work you are doing, people who need a lot of short, quick interactions with colleagues will want to spend a lot of their time in this kind of space.

Contrasting to commons is the cave. This is a quiet space with minimal interruptions where deep work can happen. Nowadays, this is often people's home working environment, but it can also be a booked room in the office or, for a lucky few, an office of their own. If people are trying to do deep work in a common space, you should spot this and offer them an alternative quiet area where they will be able to concentrate.

Collaboration

The third of your environment options is the collaboration space. A lot of people spend a lot of time in meetings, and very often those meetings are poorly run and inefficient. We'll talk more about running effective meetings later in the book, but if you think of those interactions where multiple people need to come together for discussion, brainstorming, decision-making etc., as areas for collaboration, then you might get more out of them. A collaboration space should be used reasonably sparingly as you are bringing a lot of resources together to focus on a particular topic or task, but it is where you will get the most out of your team and stakeholders working together. Your collaboration space should be equipped with whiteboards, flip charts, Post-It Notes, and timers.

One of the best locations for work that people often miss is a space for contemplation. We have brilliant brains, if we could just let them do their work, but too often the urgent buzz of the office or the constant ping of emails and meetings prevents us from giving the big questions and challenges proper thought. That's why impactful project managers deliberately schedule time for contemplation, in an environment that is conducive to it. Many people will say that their best ideas come to them in the shower, or when driving their car or lying in bed at night. The common thing about all these areas is that there is nothing else competing for the processing power of your thinking brain. When you get rid of the noise and allow your brain to do its work, the results can be astounding!

You will make better decisions, direct better work efforts for your team, solve thorny problems, and figure out why things are going wrong if you just take the time to stand-back and think about things.

I find that swimming, walking, riding a bike, and taking a bath are all highly effective ways of allowing your brain to think. So why not take a bit more control of the situation and schedule these things into your working day? That's right – your working day! Between 9 a.m. and 5:30 p.m.! If you do this for a couple of hours a week and direct your thoughts towards your most challenging problems, I assure you that the time will be well spent! It might be a step too far to install a bath in your corporate HQ, but blocking out an hour for a walk to really think through a problem can be a highly effective use of your time, and a great way to get some extra exercise in during the working day.

Contemplation – time to think, learn, and solve problems

If you want to make your contemplation time even more effective, then there is an added technique that I use all the time to get ideas for the various challenges in work. I make a conscious decision about what I am feeding my brain! If I am about to go into a big negotiation, then I buy or re-listen to an audio book about negotiation like Fisher & Ury's famous *"Getting to yes"*. If I'm figuring out how to roll-out significant change in an organisation, then an audiobook like Chip & Dan Heath's *"Switch"* is very helpful or if I'm struggling to understand a person's point of view then *"Surrounded by idiots"* by Thomas Erikson is a great listen. The key here is that I am making a deliberate decision to feed my brain useful ideas and techniques that relate to the specific work I am doing or problem that I'm facing. I almost always come up with a new idea or get a suggestion from the author on how I can move things forward. Try it for just a few hours – it's life-changing!

All these spaces are useful for certain types of work, and trying to do the wrong kind of work in the wrong environment is frustrating and wasteful. Have a look at your diary for the week and figure out for you and your team what work should be done in which environment. Then do what you can to make sure that you are planning the right work in the right location.

If your team is working remotely, something simple like an office day once a week, or even once a month, can help a remote team work much more effectively. You can make an office day even more impactful if you can use a couple of hours of that day to have a great workshop on an important subject. If your balance is the other way and the company culture is such that everyone is in the office every day, you could perhaps find ways to give people that dedicated quiet time to get their heads down and work with no distractions. This could be as simple as booking a meeting room for a few hours to use as a dedicated 'quiet room', where no one is allowed to talk, only to work on their tasks. As an impactful project manager, it's your job to think this through and come up with a solution that works for your team.

Different workers need different balances of workspace. Even for highly focused workers like software developers or accountants, there are benefits to spending some time in a common space where they can pick up information through osmosis. In other words, team members pick up elements of what is going on in the project, the company, and the wider world by overhearing other conversations and by being pulled into sidebar chats. Don't underestimate the value of this kind of communication but do make sure that you are managing it and deciding how much of it should happen. Here are some examples of the kinds of work that are best in each kind of environment.

- Cave work
  - Coding
  - Writing a report
  - Detailed spreadsheet analysis
  - Reviewing someone's work
  - Research
- Commons work
  - Training new team members
  - Help desks
  - General work – replying to emails etc.
- Collaboration work
  - Brainstorming ideas
  - Developing the project plan
  - Identifying risks
  - Estimating work (more on this later)
- Contemplation work
  - Problem solving
  - Creative ideas
  - Focused thought

Facilitating Meetings

If you are going to be an impactful project manager, it is crucial that you can get the very best out of the time you are spending with team members and stakeholders. It is heart-breaking to see how much time is wasted in poorly run meetings.

Just by putting in the effort to facilitate your meetings properly, you can significantly increase both the productivity of your project, and the credibility of your project management skills. One of the most common frustrations of project teams is that they are 'wasting their time' in too many meetings. This is typically because the meetings that they expected to attend are not well facilitated and end up having too many or the wrong people in them.

Project managers are generally the people who set up meetings, and just 10 minutes spent on planning the meeting properly and making sure that you have clear goals for it will shift your meetings into the top 10% of facilitated meetings that your team and stakeholders will attend. Your colleagues will really appreciate this, and your project will run much more smoothly and effectively.

The HiPPO (Highest-Paid Person's Opinion)

Whatever your role in a project, you will find yourself in workshops and meetings where ideas are discussed. Unfortunately, there is a very dangerous animal lurking in such places. The Highest-Paid Person's Opinion (or HiPPO) is one of the most damaging guests in a meeting. In my former life as a CIO, I was acutely aware that my opinion was one of the most dangerous things to share at the start of any meeting where I was the most senior person. Let me explain.

Every workplace has a complex ecosystem of relationships, reporting lines, and influences. One of the most interesting parts of many of our jobs is the so-called 'office politics'. 'He said this', 'she did that' is very often what is talked about at the proverbial water cooler, at lunch, or over the partitions of our desks. As people become more senior in organisations, not only does their voice carry more weight by dint of their title, but they also get more and more confident that they know all the answers. Interestingly, while it is true that they often have good ideas about solutions to problems, as people become more senior, they get less and less information about the details of what is going on at the grass-roots level. Often the opinions of people on the front line are critical to the discussion, and their ideas can be quite hard to get out of them in a public forum, especially if the highest-paid (or most senior, knowledgeable or vocal) person has already expressed their opinion.

We've all been there. We're in a meeting with a more senior person and a topic comes up that we have some ideas about. Just as we are about to say something, someone more senior/confident/knowledgeable jumps in and makes a different point. We know that they are wrong, or that there is a better way to do something, but we don't say anything because to do so would be to publicly challenge them and the consequences of doing so could be unfavourable. So, the idea remains unsaid, the project goes off in a different direction, and value is left on the table.

You will want the input of the confident people, but you also need the input of everyone else. I recommend actively removing the HiPPO from the early parts of the discussion using the techniques below.

Tame the HiPPO

Taming the HiPPO is a real skill. If you are the highest-paid person (HiPP), then the self-control to let other people go first is quite difficult to master. If you are not the HiPP, the person who is the HiPP probably has a lot of influence over your career. They may set your goals and objectives; they may be a strong influencer on your boss; or they may be someone who can damage the project if they are not onboard. So, what can you do to tame the HiPPO? There are three very powerful techniques that I use very regularly.

1 – Let the HiPP know about the danger of their O(pinion)

If you can take that person for a coffee and have a chat about this subject, you will often find that they are quite flattered to be considered such a strong influencer of other people's opinions. With some tact and diplomacy, you might even be able to convince them of the value of letting everyone else get their opinions out on the table first. You can reassure them that their opinion will be included in the discussion. If you really develop your diplomacy skills, you might even open them up to being more interested in what other people in the meeting are saying, and perhaps even give them a way of changing their opinions while saving face. I have found that, contrary to the common perception, most senior people nowadays have very high levels of emotional intelligence. Upon being given the opportunity (in a non-public environment) to think about the influence they have on other people, they are usually very open to engaging with facilitation techniques that give everyone's opinions and ideas equal weight. Having this conversation can be a great way to build your relationship with a senior leader, show your own empathy, and demonstrate the effectiveness of your own project management techniques.

2 – Capture everything before anything is said – Silent Writing

This is one of the most powerful facilitation techniques I have ever come across, and it is extremely simple. The power of the technique lies in the fact that once an idea or opinion is written down, it is safe. Once someone has taken the time to put pen to paper after thinking about a subject or question, the idea is not only likely to be worthwhile, but it will also not disappear in the face of alternate ideas – even if those are provided by the dreaded HiPPO. Silent writing is something that is alien to many 'brainstorming' sessions. Often people just start shouting out ideas, and only the loudest voices get heard or the session runs out of time before all the ideas have been captured.

In a facilitated session with silent writing, there is no risk of the ideas being lost because they all end up on sticky notes (see the below note on Post-it notes). The technique is simple.

1. You ask the question and write it on a whiteboard or flip chart.
2. Give everyone a stack of Post-it notes and a sharpie.
3. Then you set the timer for three to five minutes and enforce silence for that time while everyone writes their ideas down.

When I say silence, I mean absolute silence, exam conditions, no talking, no looking at each other's answers, no checking phones or laptops, just writing one idea after another on sticky notes. During this time, I tend to walk around the room and make a joke about being an "invigilator". Everybody has been in an exam, and once you enforce these conditions for everybody, no one feels singled out. It is only a few minutes, but you can generate tens or even hundreds of ideas this way, and the great thing is that if you go back and collect all the Post-It Notes and get people to read them out, all the ideas will be captured. Of course, there will be some overlap and some crazy ideas, but these are useful in themselves as they can start to show consensus or creativity.

Silent writing

If you like, you can play music in the background while the silent writing is taking place (I like Shakira's 'Try Everything' to really get the creative juices flowing), but if you stick to the exam conditions, everyone will not only get a fair chance to have their ideas captured, but they will also walk away feeling that they did. This feeling is going to be useful later when you are building the consensus around your next steps.

3 – Use the power of the parking lot

Another problem with the HiPPO or other loud voices in any meeting is that they sometimes get off track in terms of the meeting's goals. Someone may have a burning issue, and this is the only time they feel they are likely to get all the right people into a room to listen to them. They may be frustrated with something or there might be an outstanding topic from the last meeting that needs resolving. As a result, they hijack your meeting to resolve their issue. These hijackings of the conversation are often extremely important – at least to the person who is making the point – so they need to be handled sensitively but shouldn't be allowed to take over the meeting. As a facilitator, this is one of the hardest things to deal with.

Fortunately, there is a great technique to bring the discussion back on track very easily. It requires only a tiny amount of prep but gives you a huge amount of control over keeping the meeting on the right subject.

At the start of the meeting, you simply put a piece of flip chart paper or even a couple of sticky notes on a wall with the title 'Parking Lot'. You tell everyone what it is for, and then you get on with the meeting. When the meeting looks like it is at risk of being hijacked, you simply let the conversation go on for as long as you feel is appropriate (two or three minutes is normally about right) and then you step in with a comment along the lines of 'This sounds really important. Let's capture it in the parking lot and make sure to carry on this conversation at the right time with all the right people.'

Of course, you then have an action to make sure that the conversation does get picked up and continued, but taking action is a huge part of being a project manager, and you now have control of both conversations. Everyone feels like their points have been heard and taken seriously and your meeting can continue with the planned agenda without being derailed.

How to maintain control of a meeting

A Note on Post-it Notes

When I finished university, I spent two months in the rainforests of Borneo planting trees to replace the ones that had been taken by loggers. We lived in hammocks in a camp in the jungle surrounded by ants, snakes, leeches, scorpions, and biting insects of all types. There was a myriad of dangers, from falling trees to flash floods and food poisoning. It was backbreaking work. Our days consisted of carrying uncomfortable metal cages full of saplings on our backs in the heat, stopping every 20 metres or so, and digging holes with a *cangkul* (Malaysian for hoe). Then we would slit the little plastic wrapper off the sapling's roots, drop the sapling into the hole, cover it over with soil, and water it. We suffered leech bites, swarming bees in the middle of our camp, and a memorable encounter with a Sumatran pit viper called Cecil. After two months of work, our team of 25 people had planted in the region of 20,000 trees. Those trees are still there, in the protected Danum Valley Nature Reserve in Malaysian Borneo, and are growing every day, sucking CO_2 out of the atmosphere and providing habitat for thousands of animals and plants in one of the most threatened parts of our planet.

Why do I tell you this? Because I have a habit that is not as environmentally friendly as I would like. *I LOVE Post-it notes.* They are possibly the most versatile, underused, powerful tool in a project manager's arsenal. They allow a single person to gather ideas and data from a whole room full of people in just a few minutes. They allow you to group that data and sort it so that trends come to life. They help everyone in the room to have an equal voice. Most importantly, they do all this for a very reasonable price when compared to all the other project management tools ever invented.

There are a few rules that apply when it comes to using Post-it notes. I often explain these rules at the start of a facilitated session to add a bit of humour into the room and to make sure that people use the Post-it notes correctly. These rules also have the added value of allowing you to bring some comedy back into the discussion later in the session when someone inevitably uses a Post-it note incorrectly.

Rule 1 – There is an art to peeling Post-it notes (This is best demonstrated with actions).
If you grab it by the bottom and lift it up quickly, the sticky part of the Post-it note gets curled up. When you try to stick it to the wall, it's already lost part of its stickiness and is more likely to fall off the wall and end up on the floor. The correct way to peel a Post-it note is by carefully lifting on one side, just below the sticky part, and then gently peeling across. This way, the Post-it note keeps its true form and is much less likely to end up on the floor or stuck to the bottom of someone's shoe. Now, everybody, take a pile of Post-it notes and try it together . . . . See what I mean?! Life-changing, I tell you.

Rule 2 – Only one idea per Post-it note.
We are going to be moving these notes around and clustering them into groups. You'll need to take them away at the end for the all-important write-up. If people write more than one idea on a Post-it note, you'll have to rip them when the ideas need to be used in different ways. One of the parts will not have the little sticky bit on the back and will end up on the floor and that idea could be lost forever.

Rule 3 – The ideas should be written concisely and make sense on their own without context.
For the same reasons as rule 2, the ideas will not necessarily end up in the same order and may need to be interpreted on their own, so keep it brief and make sure it makes sense without being next to anything else.

Rule 4 – Write on the correct side of the Post-it note.
This should be obvious, but you would be surprised how many people write on the sticky side of Post-it notes. This leads to significant problems with having to fold over the top of the Post-it note to get it stuck on the wall with the words facing outwards, and all of a sudden, you have lost part of the writing and are (once again!) more likely to end up with Post-it-to-floor contact.

Rule 5 – Sticky at the top please.
The elegant design of a Post-it note is perfect if it is used with the sticky bit at the top. However, some philistines find it necessary to write on a Post-it note with the sticky on the side or (horror of horrors) with the sticky bit on the bottom! This ruins the symmetry of your Post-it note display and can also lead to Post-it-on-the-floor syndrome.

Optional Rule 6 – FOR ADVANCED POST-IT NOTE USERS ONLY!!!
There is a final way that is even better than the peel-from-the-side technique. If you are a confident Post-it note user and you have a decently sized stack of notes, you may, on occasion, use the 'pull-down' technique. This gives a perfectly flat Post-it note, but you must make sure that your stack is big enough. Trying the pull-down technique on a small stack of Post-it notes will not only often end in a very curled-up Post-it but could potentially damage the rest of the stack.

Using post-it notes

These rules, if delivered correctly, can start your session off with a bit of humour and let everyone know that you are there to have a bit of fun as well as get down to the serious business of the meeting. I tend to use increasing urgency as I go through the rules so that people can really get a flavour of my love for Post-it notes and my frustration when they are used incorrectly. I finish with a smile, and we can all move on to the serious business of the icebreaker.

A note on my note about Post-it notes: Despite being one of Post-it's best customers and having taught these techniques to hundreds of people, I still do not have a sponsorship deal with 3M, the makers of Post-it notes. If anyone knows anyone who can facilitate the discussion between myself and this great company, I would be very grateful for an introduction. 😉

Agendas

How many meetings that you go to have an agenda? Ten percent? Five percent? Even fewer? While agendas are quite common for very senior meetings like steering and board meetings, very few people bring that discipline back to the more regular and frequent meetings of the week. I think this is because, very often, people simply don't spend the time and effort to really figure out what the meeting's purpose is supposed to be. Just that little bit of planning and then stating the goals of the meeting up-front will transform the meeting's productivity and value.

An agenda can be very simple and unchanging or quite complicated and well thought through. For most meetings, something simple is best, but when you have a large group or are trying to do something complicated, using specific techniques throughout the meeting and keeping it going are powerful skills to deploy.

The Most Basic Agenda

If you find yourself with a regular meeting that you want to impose a bit of structure on, I can highly recommend stealing the format of the daily stand-up from Scrum. This is a great way for everyone to get a sense of what everyone else is doing, raise the issues that need to be dealt with, and use people's time effectively. All you do is go around the room, giving everyone the chance to describe the following three questions:

1. What I did yesterday
2. What I'm doing today
3. Any blockers or risks

That's it.

Once you get good at this, you'll be able to do it with a team of five to six people in about 15 minutes, and it will give you great control over the project. It gives you visibility of what the team members are working on, helps everyone to align, gives the opportunity for people to ask for and offer help, and makes it clear what you need to do as the project manager to move impediments out of the team's way.

The 'Build-as-You-Go' Agenda

Another great way to build an agenda is to look at the meetings in your diary for the next week and put a heading in your notebook with space to take notes on topics that should be on the agenda for that meeting. I find this particularly effective for one-to-one meetings (1:1s), either with my own line manager or with individual team members. By creating that space to take a note on what you should be discussing with someone next time you meet, you are able to consolidate all the different activities and thoughts from the week or month into one list that can quickly be prioritised and tidied up before the meeting. This is great because it means you are using both your time and the time of the person you are meeting very effectively, and you are much less likely to forget to mention something important. It also has the massive benefit of reducing the likelihood of interruptions the rest of the time. If you know you have a 1:1 in a couple of days, and that you will get a chance to talk face to face with your colleague about whatever just crossed your mind, you will be much less likely to feel the need to interrupt them in what they are doing when the thought occurs to you.

If you can encourage everyone on the team to do this for their regular meetings (mainly 1:1s and team meetings) then you will quickly find that progress becomes smoother and fewer things get missed.

Icebreakers

Getting people to engage with a meeting can be hard. Silent writing is a powerful tool for getting ideas, and it is made even stronger if people have spoken at least once already in the meeting. The best way to make sure this happens is by using icebreakers.

There are very many different icebreakers that you can choose out there. My favourites ensure that people get to talk about something uncontroversial, which they are confident about and happy to share with the group. As I regularly facilitate meetings, I have invested in a large supply of Play-Doh, but you can get a similar result by asking people to draw a picture on a Post-it. Simply give everyone a hunk of Play-Doh or a Post-it note, set a timer for two minutes, and ask them to make or draw something that people in the room might not know about them.

Then go around the room giving people a minute or two to introduce themselves and explain their model/drawing. Because the models and drawings are almost all quite basic and often unrecognisable, this is another way to get a bit of humour into the room. Your job is to make sure that everyone gets to share their art but also to follow up with a few questions to get the conversation going. If someone is interested in knitting, ask them what they are currently working on. If they coach a football team, ask them when the next match is and how the preparations are going. Having human conversations at the start of a meeting can break down barriers and make the rest of the meeting much more productive and fun.

Play-Doh icebreaker

You are probably not going to run an icebreaker for regular meetings or where everyone already knows each other well because people will see it as a waste of time, but the principle of having a human conversation still applies. Ask a few questions about people's interests or personal lives in the chit-chat at the start of the meeting, and you'd be surprised how you can manage the mood of the room, even if the upcoming agenda is very serious or controversial.

In Meetings

Your behaviour in the meetings themselves will determine whether that meeting is effective or not. As the project manager, it's often your job to facilitate the meeting to make sure that it achieves its purpose, and that everyone walks away impressed and happy. No easy task!

However, if you have been organised before the meeting and set up an agenda and a parking lot (if you think it's likely that the meeting will be side-tracked), invited the right people (and only the right people), and had the relevant preparatory discussions, you will at least be starting in a good place. From that good start, though, things can go downhill. Timing (or time-boxing) is a real skill that requires practice and focus. You will have to figure out from your own context how much time to spend on each topic, but I recommend that you look at the agenda before the meeting and allocate a rough time to each point either mentally or explicitly. Many meetings never get to the important discussions, either because there is too much on the agenda or because the facilitator is not strong enough on driving the conversation forwards.

Impactful project managers are not afraid to push the meeting forwards. If the meeting is about a decision, then make sure that decision gets made. If the meeting is to inform people, make sure that the most important pieces of information are discussed. It is not rude to move a meeting along if it's done sensitively and in the right way.

Timers

If I feel like there is a risk of poor timing, I will go to the extent of using a kitchen timer in a meeting. I say at the beginning that there are some important points scheduled for later in the meeting, so to keep us on track, I am setting a timer for X minutes for each part of the discussion. Some people might do this poorly and come across as rude, but I've found that if you talk about this up-front and with a bit of humour and explain that you see it as your job to make sure everyone's time is being valued, then you can get buy-in for this approach from almost any group. Once you've agreed to set a time limit on a discussion, the timer becomes the 'bad guy' when it's time to move on – not you! Of course, you'll need to read the room. You don't want someone to feel like an important point has not been discussed properly or that they have been cut off without a chance to speak, but by using the parking lot and the timer sensitively, you should find it much easier to navigate those issues and people will appreciate your efforts for making the best use of their time.

A timer can be too formal or inappropriate for some meetings, but you can achieve a lot of the same results through your own behaviour. You can do this simply by having a clear time frame in your own mind, taking a quick glance at your watch at the appropriate time, and saying, 'We need to move on so that we get a chance to discuss x.' Whichever way you choose, be clear in your mind that it is your job to make sure the meeting goes well and achieves its goals. No one else is going to do it for you!

Getting Ideas – The SAVE Technique

I strongly advocate the idea of having a toolkit of techniques that you use in your projects, and sometimes you come across a set of tools that just work beautifully together. This is how I feel about three techniques silent writing, affinity clustering, and voting. I call using these together the SAVE approach (**S**ilent writing, **A**ffinity Clustering, **V**ote, **E**xecute).

In project management you often find yourself with a need to get input from your team on a complex question. If you can get that input effectively so that everyone is heard and then build the input into themes which are then prioritised in terms of importance, you have a powerful way of engaging the best skills and knowledge of your team or stakeholders to almost any problem.

Here's how you do it:

Step 1 – Silent writing

Write the question you are trying to answer on a flip chart or whiteboard, give everyone Post-it notes and sharpies and set a timer for three minutes. No talking, just writing (make sure you have explained the rules of using Post-it notes first).

Step 2 – Affinity clustering

Once the timer goes off, you ask each person to bring their Post-it notes up to you one at a time and read them out on the way. As you take the Post-it from them, you stick it on the wall. If it is the first time that topic has come up, you start a new section on the wall. If someone else has already said something similar, you group the notes together to form a cluster.

In this way, you bring all the ideas up on to the wall, and you will see themes start to emerge of what people think about the topic.

Affinity clustering

Step 3 – Voting

The affinity clustering will give you the topic's themes, but not necessarily show the importance of each one. If you then ask each person to put three to five 'votes' on the themes and use the votes to rank the themes by importance to the topic at hand, you will very easily be able to create a prioritised list. You can use those little sticky dots from the stationary cupboard, or you can just get people to draw a dot with their pen for each vote.

You have now extracted all the best thoughts from your group, clustered them into themes, and developed an idea of the prioritisation of those themes – all in just a few minutes, and much more efficiently than most other brainstorming techniques. You have used people's time effectively, given everyone a chance to be heard, and created a tangible action plan to work on.

Step 4 – Execute

Now you discuss as a team what the next steps are going to be, who is going to write-up the list, and what you are going to do with the top priority tasks on the list. This might be another, more detailed workshop, a discussion with a stakeholder who wasn't in the room, or just some work that the team start going with. This is crucial as it is remarkable how many great brainstorming sessions end up with no write-up and no actions. Do not be the project manager who facilitates a brilliant brainstorming session and then fails to execute any of the insights and actions that come out of it.

The SAVE technique is an invaluable way to start many of the key actions of project management. From developing a risk log to identifying tasks that need to be completed to figuring out ideas for the team away-day, I have used these techniques together countless times, and I get an impressive outcome and buy-in from the participants every time.

Writing It Up

Now that you have these ideas from everyone, it is time to do one of the least popular but most important jobs of a project manager: write it up!

By spending 30 minutes immediately after the meeting writing up all those Post-it notes and clusters into a proper document (plan, risk log, word cloud), you suddenly make it all tangible. I am amazed at how often people fail to take this simple action from workshops. If you don't spend those few minutes turning the input into something real, you are missing one of the most impactful opportunities to manage your project that is available to you. Human nature means that leaving something for later very often means that it doesn't get done at all, and every hour that you leave the write-up after the meeting makes the whole process less and less effective.

It's easy to force yourself to do this as well. Just block out time for writing up the outcomes and updating the relevant documents immediately after the meeting when you set up the meeting itself. If you have a time-block in your diary for write-up either immediately after the meeting, or later that day, you can keep that time reserved for making sure you get full value out of the amazing meeting you just had. Be strong - do not let it get bumped by something more urgent; write-ups are best done as soon after the brainstorm as possible.

Lean Coffee

Sometimes, a meeting's purpose isn't to create output. It is just to help people discuss whatever is on their minds and get some support. In this case, you can use the lean coffee technique.

This follows the basic set-up as the SAVE approach, but by asking for questions instead of answers, you can create an agenda for the meeting that is developed entirely by the people in the meeting, then addresses their concerns in priority order. This leads to amazing coaching and problem-solving discussions. There is a slight tweak you need to make to SAVE to turn it into a lean coffee session.

1. Set the topic – e.g. What is not working well for the team at the moment? I find that for Lean Coffee, quite a broad topic is best.
2. Silent writing – this time you are only looking for 1-3 topics per person that people want to discuss.
3. Get the Post-it notes on the wall – Just like affinity clustering, each person reads out their topic and brings it up. This time though, you are not looking quite so hard for groupings; you want to make sure that everyone's questions are called out and everyone has a chance to state the importance of their topic.
4. Voting – Everyone votes for the topic that is most important to them. Give everyone 1, 3, or 5 votes depending on the size of the group. Smaller groups have more votes per person. They can allocate their votes all to one topic or spread them out amongst a few.
5. Prioritise the list – The topic with the highest number of votes goes at the top, ranking down to the one with the lowest number of votes at the bottom.

6. Once you have your prioritised list, you set a timer for three to five minutes and start talking about the most important question. The person who raised the topic explains a bit more about it, and then you facilitate a positive discussion on it.
7. When the timer goes off, everyone votes with their hand in a Roman gladiator style on whether you should keep talking about that topic or move on to the next one:

   - Thumbs up = keep talking about this topic
   - Thumb horizontal = don't know
   - Thumb down = I think we're finished, let's move on to the next one

The power of this is that you can cover a lot of ground quite quickly or get into detailed conversations on important topics if the group feels it is the need to do so.

I often finish up a team meeting with lean coffee for 20 to 30 minutes as a great way to get any hot topics out into the open and give the group advice and ideas on how to solve whatever issue is on their minds.

Drawing Pictures

The best way to communicate is face to face. You pick up a lot from body language, tone of voice, and context that you would miss on a video call or phone call. Don't get me started on the terrible communication that can happen over email; we'll deal with that later in the book. Even stronger than face-to-face communication is face-to-face communication with a whiteboard to draw on. The human brain is highly adapted to processing visual images. It had millions of years of evolution to improve visual processing but has spent much less time developing speech and only a tiny fraction of the time dealing with written language. By some estimates, over 60% of the brain is involved in processing visual material one way or another.

This is why Tais and I have put so much effort into the illustrations throughout this book. If we can explain something visually, there is a much better chance of you understanding it, remembering it, and using it. The same applies to your own interactions with your colleagues. If you can spend a little bit more time with a whiteboard marker in your hand and use images to help you discuss problems, then you are using the tools you have much more effectively. Whether it's a mind map, system diagram, creative matrix, or simply a picture of a few cars to bring the 'parking lot' to life, you will rarely regret spending the time on turning ideas into images to aid your discussions. It will bring the conversation to life, identify gaps in your understanding, and help everyone to remember what was talked about.

Tais is extremely talented and has worked hard to develop her skills, and hopefully you will see the benefit of her illustrations, but even I – with no formal training and not one iota of natural talent – use drawings like this all the time in workshops and discussions. If you are worried that you can't draw, I can highly recommend a 15-minute YouTube video by Graham Shaw entitled, 'Why People Believe They Can't Draw – and How to Prove They Can'.

Language

How you speak as a project manager matters. Your phrases and idiosyncrasies can have a big impact. You may not realise it but giving constructive feedback can come across as micro-managing or nit-picking. Nobody thinks they are micro-managing anybody, and yet many people feel like they are being micro-managed. Nobody thinks they are criticising someone else, but people feel criticised all the time.

There are no magic solutions to this problem, it is something that comes with experience, trust, and time, but there are a couple of things that I like to bear in mind when it comes to language.

Above all, be positive. One of the first pieces of feedback I ever received in my first job was that I was enthusiastic and positive. That stuck with me and became part of not only who I was, but also who I wanted to be. Being positive, optimistic, and enthusiastic costs nothing and it makes people enjoy interacting with you much more. There are no problems in business that have not been solved or resolved a thousand times. There is always a way of moving something forward or making a situation better, so before you have a conversation, have a think about how you can make it a positive one.

The second point that is worth having in mind is that there are some very powerful phrases which open conversations much more than others. Phrases like 'How might we . . .?', 'Tell me about . . .' and 'I was really impressed by . . .' are simple additions to your daily phraseology that can make a very large and positive difference to your interactions with colleagues. Try to use them a bit more each day and they will become more and more natural as you grow in your interactions.

Now you have a few powerful techniques, let's look at some of the general approaches that are used by project managers to set some structure around their projects.

Chapter 4
Approach – Some Ideas on How to Structure Your Project

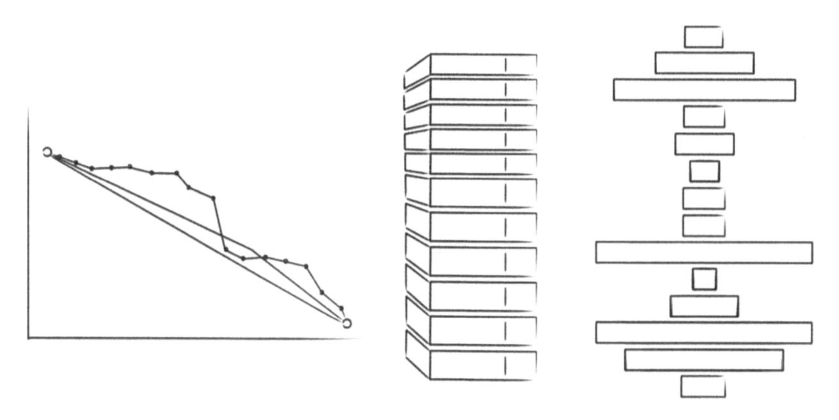

Pick the right method for the right moment

There are as many ways to manage a project as there are projects. Whether your organisation follows PMI, PRINCE2, Scrum, Kanban, SAFe, LeSS, Lean, some combination of these, something else, or nothing at all, you will still have to deliver the project. I would recommend that you think about your project delivery approach in the context of three things:

- The organisation you are working in.
- The team and stakeholders you are working with.
- The project you are working on.

Some organisations (usually large ones) have highly defined methodologies, with stage gates and governance structures that need to be followed. In these organisations, your job is to understand this methodology and make it work for you. Other organisations have very little in the way of artefacts and governance and you may have a free reign to run the project how you see fit. The key thing to remember is that all these different approaches have pros and cons. If you can understand your organisation and use what is there to make your life easier, keep stakeholders happy, and deliver the project, that's great. If you can take what is there and sprinkle some of the tools and techniques in this book on top to make it more effective, so much the better. Unless you are setting up a project management office (PMO) from scratch, fighting against what the organisation already has in place is rarely worth doing. You are going to have to work with the system and make the best of it.

https://doi.org/10.1515/9783111271149-004

There is good news, though. The big frustration that I mentioned at the start of the book, about how generic project management methodologies are rarely perfect for any given project, is something that you can use to your advantage. The fact that they are generic makes them quite flexible and gives you control as a project manager if you are prepared to take it.

In organisations where the PMO is 'mature', they very often have lots of artefacts and processes that need to be followed. They might have a certain format they expect status reports to be delivered in, or they might expect project plans to be presented in a certain way. While this might create a bit of administration overhead, it absolutely does not prevent you from using any of the techniques in this book if you are proactive, creative, and sensible about it.

For example, many organisations have a certain format for the RAID log (Risks, Assumptions, Issues, and Dependencies). Some project managers see this as an overhead, an annoyance. They know their project and they are managing their risks, so why should they write them down? I would argue that this is simply one tool in the toolbox and so get on and use it. The PMO will not prevent you from running a SAVE workshop to identify your RAID items. They will just expect them to be written up in a certain way. The key to making this a positive rather than a negative is to include the work of maintaining and updating the necessary documentation in your estimates of the project. If you need a junior project manager to help you because the PMO expects 24 different project artefacts, include that in your estimates and plans and make sure that your stakeholders are aware of all the writing-up work that is going on. If the organisation's senior management don't realise the cost of maintaining a large body of documentation, they will keep adding to it.

If you feel like your organisation has lost the run of itself and is asking for lots of things that are not adding value, you can always share this book with a few people. When I work with large organisations on reviewing their methodologies, we often find huge waste in their processes and documentation, you are not alone, and things can be done, but your focus has to be on delivering your project, not boiling the ocean!

Rather than getting frustrated with the way things are done, and if it feels like revamping your organisation's whole approach is beyond your remit (and energy levels), the best thing to do may well be to understand what's required and then make sure that you are making the processes work as well as possible for your project. With that in mind, let's touch on a few of the main approaches for delivering projects.

Waterfall Delivery

In a waterfall project, you only go through each phase of the project once. It used to be the only way that most projects were managed, and it created a lot of work for consultants (myself included) – a lot of which was wasted. The basic idea is that you define all the requirements up-front. You have workshops with stakeholders, talk about it a lot, and write it all down. Then you go through a design phase where you figure out how the requirements will be delivered, which ones are critical, and which ones can be removed. Then you move on to a build phase where the whole product is built in one go. Then you test everything and fix any issues. After all that, you put the product live.

Waterfall delivery

Waterfall projects work fine for well-understood builds where there is a lot of experience and very little risk in the project. Everyone knows exactly what they want up-front, and there are other constraints (like long lead times on materials) that mean decisions must be made in advance.

A great place to use waterfall project management is in building a house. You can imagine how difficult it would be to change something fundamental about the design of a house late in the project, and you need to order materials weeks, sometimes months in advance. Building a house is also a relatively well-understood project. The people doing the work are experts in what they do, and they have done it many times before. When they think through a problem, they can see all the angles based on their experience, and they have developed a tried and tested order of activities that gets the job done every time.

1. Site preparation
2. Laying the foundations
3. Building the superstructure
4. Building the wall plate
5. Building the roof
6. First fix: carpentry and exteriors
7. First fix: plumbing and electrics
8. Drainage and external works
9. Preparing ceilings/dry linings
10. Second fix: carpentry
11. Second fix: electrics and plumbing
12. Decorating
13. Landscaping
14. Cleaning and snagging

Each of these stages has a checklist of activities that need to be done at that stage to avoid problems later in the build. You don't decorate the walls before you've completed the carpentry because if you did, there would be damage to the decoration, and you'd have to do it again. Those of us who are DIY enthusiasts, but not skilled in the building trade, are very aware of that 'oops' moment when you have done something in the wrong order and must either take it apart again or redo some work because you didn't think of a problem that was coming down the line. It's extremely frustrating and wasteful to find out that you have to go back and rework something if you think a phase is finished.

In waterfall projects, you can only start using the product when everything is done – at the very end of the project.

The tried and tested steps to building a house

This is how we used to do other projects in the world of business and technology as well. Unfortunately, there is a **huge** problem with waterfall for complex, poorly understood projects. It simply doesn't work!

To understand why not, it's useful to think about how well you know the future of your project. The housebuilder knows their project well. They have done it many times before, the ground is unlikely to change dramatically along the way, and there is only one customer, who can be coached and guided along the right path of the project.

Most of us don't have the same ability to see the future for our projects. We are working in extremely complex environments with many different influences and constraints. Many different people with different opinions can impact your project. Risks can come to pass, people can leave or make mistakes, and technology is constantly changing and adjusting. This is why, for most complex and uncertain projects, I would recommend a more agile approach.

Change Request Purgatory

If you use the waterfall approach for complex, uncertain projects, you may find yourself in a very dark place that I call Change Request Purgatory. This is not a fun place to be. You have agreed and 'signed off' all your requirements, but as soon as people see the designs, they have other ideas and request changes to what has been previously agreed. Some things get added, some things get removed, all of which require effort and cost. Then you finally get the designs signed off and you start the build. Suddenly, a competitor comes out with a new offering and your sales team thinks of a new customer feature that is absolutely required. Then a designer comes across a problem that no one thought of, and you have to change a major part of the design. Then you find that the contract negotiation with one of your vendors has thrown up a limitation on the piece of software that you were going to connect to, and now you must build that connection in a different way. Suddenly, your steering committee is looking at all these changes and the costs associated with them, and they put their foot down – no more new things without removing old things! Now you are in a review round with all your stakeholders to renegotiate the scope from the design phase and remove some of the old things, but you find that the developers have already built the foundations of some parts, and it's not worth cancelling that bit because most of the work is already done. You get the picture.

Change request purgatory

Change request purgatory is difficult to get out of. If you find yourself there, consider moving your project to a more agile methodology.

Crystal Balls

The cause of change request purgatory is people's unrealistic confidence in their own ability to see the future. As the project manager, one of your most important tasks is to spot when these unrealistic expectations are creeping in and call out 'crystal bullshit!' (get it?). We'll get to how you can manage those stakeholders in a later chapter, but for the moment, just be clear in your mind that it is your responsibility to look out for unrealistic expectations of all types, and make sure that they are brought out into the open as early as possible.

Watch out for crystal bullsh*t

In the olden days of IT project management, there used to be a thing called a requirements traceability matrix or RTM. This was one of the most painful, least effective ways to manage scope, but it was prevalent across the industry for many, many years because it gave the illusion of control.

Being in control – using PMO to hide uncertainty

Rather than really giving stakeholders control, the RTM did something quite different. It made people believe that they had thought of everything when they hadn't. Estimates, timelines, and resource plans built off the RTM were given much more credibility than they should have been. People were promised that the project would be complete in a certain timeframe, to a certain cost, with the agreed scope. And when they found out that their crystal ball was actually bullshit, what happened? Stress! For everyone involved! All those promises and plans had been baked into communications with managers, customers, and shareholders. Breaking the promises that had been made would cost everyone a lot of credibility, reputational damage and, in many cases, real money. All this stress landed back onto the project manager, who (if they weren't great at dealing with it) passed it on to their teams.

The illusion of control

This is the reason why, when I first started my career in project management, I was told that 80% of IT projects failed. This is why, as a business analyst and junior project manager I spent five years of my life in change request purgatory. It is also why I believe that, while it's a great way to build houses, waterfall is not the right approach for most complex, uncertain projects.

But thankfully, there is another way!

Agile Delivery

In February 2001, 17 visionaries got together in a ski lodge in Utah, frustrated with all the problems of waterfall project management for software development. In a creative and intense two-day session, they debated and discussed many different software delivery methodologies and the problems and advantages of each of them and distilled them down into four values and twelve principles. While these values and principles come from the world of software development, they are applicable to many of the projects that we find ourselves managing in the modern world because they are human-centric and allow for the flexibility that is needed when dealing in uncertainty.

In agile, we value:

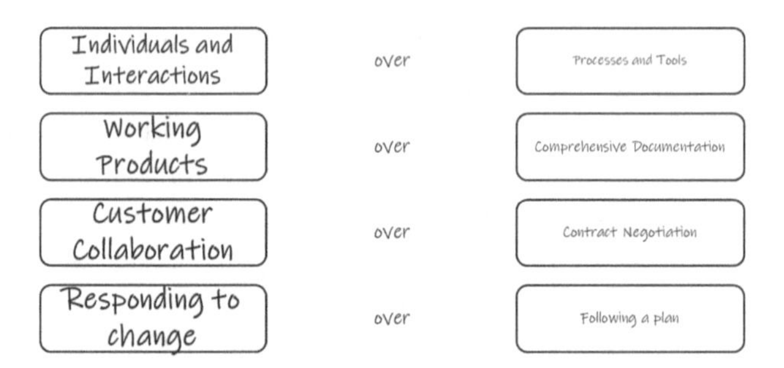

Agile manifesto values

This isn't rocket science. All the things on the left are the things we want from the project, and all the things on the right are 'traditional' ways of delivering projects. They are not bad in themselves, but when they get in the way of delivering the outcomes of the project, it becomes problematic. For many organisations trying to deliver projects consistently, they reach a point where the tail starts wagging the dog. They stop asking themselves why they are doing certain things, and just do them because they are part of the prescribed process.

On top of the agile values, these trailblazing thinkers also developed a set of principles for teams to follow that give them hints to stay on track when they are choosing how to spend their time.

Our highest priority is to satisfy the customer through **early and continuous delivery** of valuable products.	We **welcome changing requirements,** even late in development. Agile processes harness change for the customer's competitive advantage.	Deliver **working products frequently,** from a couple of weeks to a couple of months, with a preference to the shorter timescale.	Businesspeople and project team members must **work together daily** throughout the project.
Build projects around **motivated individuals.** Give them the environment and support they need, and trust them to get the job done.	The most efficient and effective method of conveying information to and within a development team is **face-to-face conversation.**	**Working products** are the primary measure of progress.	Agile processes promote **sustainable development.** The sponsors, developers, and users should be able to maintain a constant pace indefinitely.
Continuous attention to **technical excellence and good design** enhances agility.	Simplicity – the art of **maximising the amount of work not done** – is essential.	The best architectures, requirements, and designs emerge from **self-organising teams.**	At regular intervals, the team reflects on how to become more effective, then **tunes and adjusts its behaviour accordingly.**

Agile manifesto principles

These agile principles are well understood now, and there are great books and training courses out there to help you implement them in many ways. They underpin agile methodologies like Scrum, Kanban and eXtreme Programming (XP). The reason they are so popular is because they work! If you are in software development, I would highly recommend that you think carefully about getting yourself trained up in agile methodologies.

Agile projects focus on delivering something easy and valuable as quickly as possible – they call it a "minimum viable product". The goal is to produce something that works and get it out into the world to start learning from interactions with real people as soon as possible.

The minimum viable product

And then over time they add features that make the product better for the customer that build on the original product.

Adding the next most important and easiest feature

Until, after many iterations, they have created a valuable product that the customers love and have meets their actual needs and wants (rather than whatever the project team thought they would want many months ago).

And then keep making it better

This book is written for project managers who may or may not be working in software development. While there is plenty of overlap between the lenses, tips, and techniques in this book and the agile principles, and they are very often complementary, I'm hoping to give you a lot more colour and value on top of them.

What is Agile for the Rest of Us?

Agile project management, in my view, is project management that accounts for the practicalities of the real world. It takes into consideration the fact that things change over time, that our understanding of a project develops as we gain more experience, and that at no point do we know everything that can be possibly known about the project. It allows us to take calculated risks and to allocate time to experimentation and learning, and it recovers well when the rest of the world changes in unexpected ways.

Having spent many years running waterfall projects and programmes, even having a role where I was required to force people to fit in with a complex, burdensome waterfall delivery model, I have seen the huge amount of waste that is created by pretending that the world is perfect or that we have a perfect understanding of it.

In the same way that there has been a revolution in economics over the last 20 years as academics realised that people are not rational machines that make sophisticated, accurate calculations about their decisions, the revolution in project management takes people as they **are** rather than as we would like them to be. It understands that adding more work to a stressed team harms productivity; that people can only make the best decisions based on the information they have at the time; and that information can change soon after. Agile methodologies often create more successful projects precisely because they allow even the project's goals to shift over time, but actively manage them so that they continually 'course correct' to stay in line with the organisation's goals.

The other thing that is critical when it comes to project management is that there is no single right answer to the challenges and questions you will face. Successful project managers are constantly adding to a toolbox of skills, approaches, and techniques and then use their intelligence and creativity to tweak those approaches to the specific circumstances of the project they are working on. If you love the daily stand-up and time-boxing elements of Scrum but want to visualise your work using a Kanban board, great. If you think that your test team needs to work together in a 'pair programming' style as per XP because you need your new people to learn from the more experienced testers, go for it. If you have a regulatory requirement for sign-off of design documents, then overlay that into your sprint planning meetings and include it in your 'definition of ready'. Waterfall project management tells you what to do and when to do it. Impactful project management requires you to think through all the circumstances of your project and then develop an approach that is going to work for you as a team.

Another strength of impactful project management is that your approach can (and should) change over time. If something isn't working for you, then change it. If your daily 10-minute stand-ups are just too short, add five minutes, but keep the agenda tight. If people aren't working together well enough, try to find more opportunities for them to meet in informal settings, or run an icebreaker or a team event.

There are great training courses in agile delivery, and if you are using any of these methodologies, I'd highly recommend that you take yourself and your team on one to find out about it together. There are several approaches to agile delivery, but my two favourites are Scrum and Kanban.

Scrum

Scrum has become the default method for a lot of software development nowadays. It focuses on repeating a standard cadence of work known as a 'sprint'. These generally last one to four weeks and have a very defined scope that is agreed to at the beginning of the sprint by the team and stakeholders.

Scrum uses artefacts like the "Product Backlog" "Sprint Backlog" and "Definition of Done" to put some structure around the prioritisation of work. It uses "Ceremonies" like the daily stand-up, sprint planning, sprint demo, and sprint retrospective to make sure that the work is transparent and clear to everyone involved. Finally, it uses the roles to be clear about who is responsible for what. The Product Owner sets the vision for what is being achieved; the Scrum Master is the "servant Leader" of the team who removes impediments, facilitates the process, and guides the team; and there is a small team of people who actually do the work that the stakeholders want.

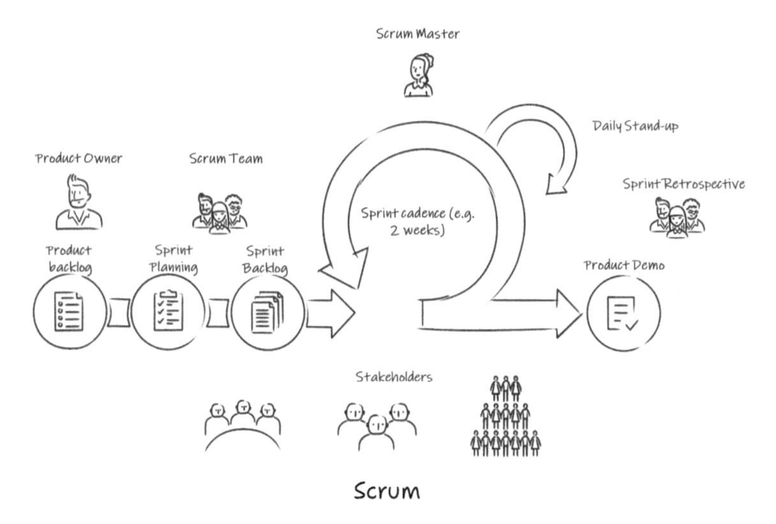

Scrum

If you want to understand Agile quickly, I can highly recommend Henrik Kniberg's YouTube video 'Agile Product Ownership in a nutshell' – he explains it beautifully in just a few minutes.

When we did the agile transformation at Cpl, I used the first 6 minutes of that video with dozens of stakeholders to help explain what we were trying to achieve. Those interactions had more impact on changing people's perception of project delivery and IT than any number of white papers and PowerPoint presentations would have had. One-on-one discussions in private where people could air their concerns and ask the "stupid" questions were the glue that held that whole transformation together. Simple, but effective!

Kanban

Kanban is all about visualisation of work and optimising the amount of work that a team or person is trying to get done at any point in time. By forcing proper decisions about prioritisation and making sure that things get finished before new things are started, Kanban is a great way to reduce the stress on your team. It's also one of the simplest approaches to explain to people. At its core, Kanban is about 3 things:

- Things we're going to do
- Things we're doing
- Things we've done.

With those three headings and a few Post-it notes with the tasks written on them or a simple piece of cloud software like Trello or Monday.com, you can transform a disorganised team that never finish a task into a productive group who tell you when they have too much work and force you to decide what they should focus on.

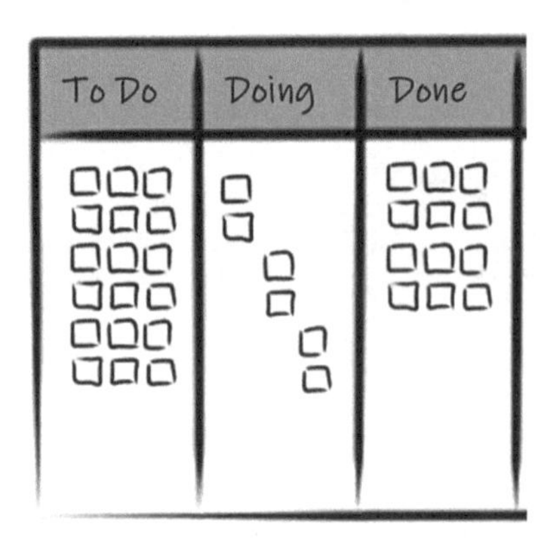

Kanban

Kanban forces you to optimise the amount of work that the team are doing at any given point so that they are productive but not overloaded. It helps you to see where the issues are and make sure that you complete work that you have committed to rather than constantly starting new work just because someone out there has asked for it.

There are many different agile approaches that are used to deliver projects. I have highlighted Scrum and Kanban as two very simple ones that can help you become an impactful project manager and can give you a very powerful structure to work from. It will be down to you to figure out your own delivery approach (or follow your organisation's), but whatever approach you follow, there is a lot that you can do to make sure that your project is successful. The methodology does not determine your project's success or failure. That will be down to you!

I would love to have spent more time explaining Scrum, Kanban, and the other agile methodologies here, but your approach to your project is only one part of your toolbox. These concepts and approaches are covered brilliantly in many other books, so I have deliberately kept it to just a high-level description here. As an impactful project manager, you will be constantly learning, so if you sign-up for Scrum training or read a book about Kanban after this one, it will be time well spent.

We now have a sense of a few of the approaches we might take and some useful tools that we can use along the way. Let's turn our attention back to those lenses and see if we can develop the sixth sense of the impactful project manager a bit more.

Chapter 5
Scope and Prioritisation – Maximise the Work that You Don't Do!

Scope is about sculpting a great outcome for your project

Scope is the 'what' of the project. It's the work that will be done, the output that will be created. It's often captured as requirements or user stories and is one of the most overlooked and poorly managed elements of many projects.

The biggest challenge with managing scope is that our understanding of it develops over time. Unless you are running a project that is very similar to one you have done in the past, the chances of being able to anticipate all the different things that the project will need to do right at the very start are vanishingly small, particularly when there is more than one organisation involved in delivering them. For many projects delivered jointly by several organisations, the start is the only time that you get to negotiate the scope because you can't start the project until the contracts have been signed, and you can't sign the contracts until everyone has agreed on what they are going to do.

This awkward dynamic creates much of the stress on projects. It sets vendor organisations who want to limit scope against buyer organisations who want to change or add to it, and it leads to a misalignment of incentives that has caused huge numbers of projects to either fail outright or be very dissatisfying for everyone involved.

Fortunately, there are ways of managing scope that can make this problem much less dangerous, and if you get it right, scope discussions can even be used to bind the team together and help trusted relationships to flourish.

At a very high level, scope management is about two things: what we are going to do and what we are not going to do. Wrestling everyone into a place where they agree on what is in and out of scope can take a lot of management and mind-reading as, unless you are explicit about scope, people will very often end up with different views and expectations.

https://doi.org/10.1515/9783111271149-005

The simplest mechanism for managing scope is to have an 'in-scope' list. This is the most basic form, and what a lot of professional project managers do (many non–project managers will not even be thinking formally about scope!). A very simple add-on to that is to have an 'out-of-scope' list to help reduce the grey areas of what is and what is not being delivered by the project. Reducing the blurry edges between what is in scope and what is out of scope is an important skill for project managers.

Minimise the blurred edges of your scope

The in-scope and out-of-scope lists can be built into a requirements traceability matrix and used to track the scope of the project throughout the different phases. Managing scope through requirements traceability is hard work and requires a lot of discussion and negotiation, but at least it can reduce the uncertainty of the project and identify areas of contention.

While this is the way that a lot of projects still work, there are much better, more human ways of managing scope than trawling through 1,000 lines of a requirements traceability matrix at the start of the project and trying to nail down every last requirement before you've even selected a partner to work with.

Prioritisation

Prioritisation is about constantly making decisions what to focus on and what to sift out

Impactful project managers see prioritisation as a huge part of managing scope. They understand that requirements can change over time, and they build mechanisms into their project to allow flexibility where it is required.

We'll talk more about it in the section on time, but the basic skill of prioritisation is to look at each piece of work with two hats on: value and effort.

Value and Effort

To figure out the relationship between value and effort, I'd like to tell you a little story. As a manager in my consulting career, I was told that to progress, I needed to be seen as an expert in something. At the time, I was working on a capital markets project, and my line manager had decided that he would make a name for himself in the technology behind certain types of complex financial derivatives. In our 1:1, he suggested that I write a white paper on a specific area of the capital markets practice so that I could then build my reputation as an expert in it. This guy was doing my appraisal, so I took his advice seriously. I went about the white paper in all the right ways. I reached out to an expert in the bank we were working with at the time and interviewed him. I found a few people in other countries who had a similar interest and read through what they'd written. I recruited a couple of more junior colleagues to help me write the paper, and we took a section each.

As you can tell by the fact that I managed to finish writing this book, I am able to get my head down and focus when I have to. So, I wrote my five sections of the paper and then set about helping the more junior colleagues with theirs and bringing the whole thing together. It was frustrating trying to get these guys to work on this "plus 1" paper as they were busy with other things, but we managed to get a draft out eventually.

I got it reviewed by my boss and by the experts in other parts of the consultancy, and after about three months of maybe five to ten hours of extra work a week, we had a nicely written paper on technology in capital markets.

While all this was going on, the project I'd been working on had come to an end, I had moved into a different area of the practice, and my line manager had changed. Trying to get the value out of the paper I'd written, I emailed it to everyone in the practice and set up a session to explain it to people. I posted it on the company's 'knowledge base' and was delighted that I'd completed a hard assignment while working full time. I was sure that it would set me apart from my peers when it came to the promotion discussions.

Unfortunately, it turns out that, despite all the effort that I'd put in, no one turned up to my meeting on the white paper and no one replied to my email. Even a year later, not one single person had read the paper on the knowledge base. The promotion discussions went ahead, and a lady who had given her full effort to the project she was working on got promoted ahead of me.

The moral of this story? The value of something rarely bears any relationship to the effort required to complete it. Some easy things are highly valuable, and some difficult things have no value at all. This is why whenever I talk about prioritisation nowadays, I always try to figure out both the value (either to myself or my company) and the effort that something is going to take. High-value, low-effort things are the best; low-value, high-effort things are the worst; and everything in between can be prioritised depending on the relative scores.

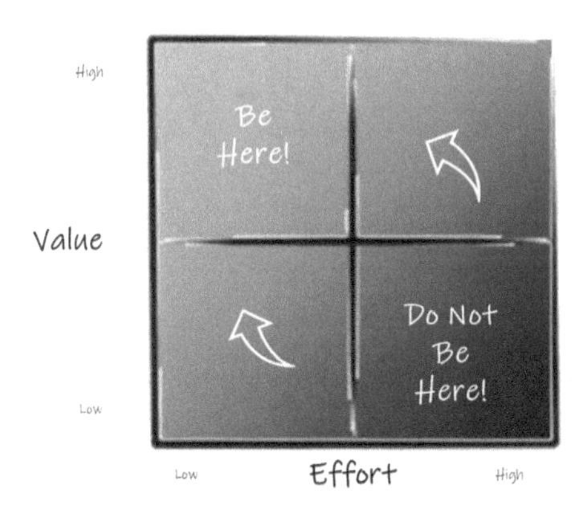

Value and effort

To further emphasise the point, imagine that our two project managers, Jill and John, have been stranded on a desert island. They are hungry and John has spotted a couple of coconuts high in a tree. He starts working hard, chopping down bamboo, making twine out of grasses, and building a complex scaffold to help him climb the coconut tree and get the food.

Meanwhile, Jill has spent a couple of hours walking around the island to see what's out there. She has come across a large pond that is teeming with fish. She grabs a stick, sharpens it, and, in a few minutes, has managed to spear several of them for their dinner.

Work on the right things

Finding yourself on in the wrong place on the value/effort matrix is very common for projects and thinking more carefully about prioritisation is one of the most effective ways that project managers can be successful. Impactful project managers always have the following thoughts in their mind:

- Just because something is easy doesn't make it low value.
- If it's hard and not valuable – don't do it!

This is a restating of the famous '80–20' rule or the 'Pareto principle' that most of the value comes from a small proportion of the work. Rather than putting specific proportions on things, I prefer to just make sure that I am always thinking about value and effort and ensuring that we are doing the right things on both axes.

Of course, we should still do some high-effort things, and some low-value things. But the high-effort things we should do are extremely valuable, and the low-value things we choose to work on should be extremely easy. As a project manager, you have a responsibility to make sure that everyone on your team is operating in this way, and that the value you get from their effort is as high as can be.

Pawpaws and Prickly Pears

As I mentioned in the Foreword to this book, I have learned a lot from the Disney movie "The Jungle Book". One of the greatest thinkers of the 20th century – Baloo the Bear – explains the concept of High Value, Low Effort beautifully in the song "the bare necessities".

> *"When you pick a pawpaw, or a prickly pear. And you prick a raw paw, well next time beware! Don't pick the prickly pear with the paw, when you pick a pear, try to use the claw! But you don't need to use the claw, when you pick a pair of the big pawpaw."*

This is such good advice that it's worth spending a bit of time on, and some nice pictures!

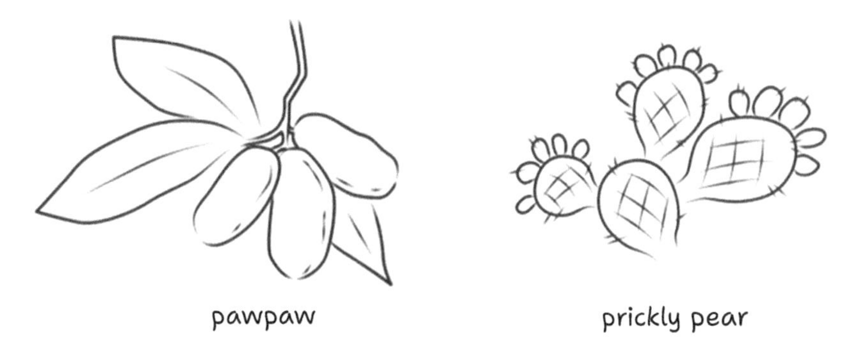

When you pick a pawpaw, or a prickly pear

And you prick a raw paw, well next time beware

Don't pick the prickly pear with a paw, when you pick a pear,
try to use the claw

But you don't need to use the claw, when you pick a pair of the big pawpaw!

As an impactful project manager, you should constantly ask yourself and your team the following questions:

- **What prickly pears are we picking** (high effort, low value work)
- If we absolutely have to pick them, **what claws could we use**? (Training, outsourcing, tools, stakeholders, delegation, escalation etc)
- **Are there any pawpaws we could be picking instead?** Stand back and look at the problem. Is there an easier solution, or a more important piece of work to do?

Prioritisation ought to be constant, it should be right at the heart of all your conversations, and you should train yourself every day to ask yourself these questions. I think we should put a lot of our effort into being more like Baloo – look for the bare necessities!

Aligning Expectations

If you are running even a moderately complex project, you will have somewhere between three and ten key stakeholders, any one of whom could derail what you are trying to do, either deliberately or inadvertently. Time spent on making sure that everyone's expectations are aligned is rarely time wasted. We'll come to ways of engaging with stakeholders in the chapter dedicated to the topic later in the book, but for now it's important to know that you need to use the right ways to engage with each person, especially when it comes to understanding and managing their expectations.

While you might have many skills as a project manager, my suspicion is that mind-reading isn't one of them. And you can be very sure that your stakeholders are not able to read *your* mind! So, while it may feel very repetitive, you need to make sure that everyone knows what they need to know about the project, and that you have also taken their views and opinions into consideration.

Being a little more formal about how you go about this can be very useful. You might not go to the extent of keeping a written tracker, but I would highly recommend that you regularly go back to your mental checklist to figure out whether there has been a change in scope that someone might need to be aware of. Looking through the 'Scope' and 'Stakeholder' lenses together, you should be able to reduce the likelihood of misaligned expectations.

Just spending time talking with stakeholders about the scope can be important. It's surprising how often they have not fully thought through a request or understood the implications of what they are asking for. By actively listening to what they are describing, playing it back to them, and asking clarifying questions, you ought to be able to get your own expectations much more closely aligned with those of your key stakeholders. If you are not spending time on this, you are behaving a bit like the proverbial ostrich with its head buried in the sand, and the misaligned expectations will come back to haunt you at some stage!

Aligning expectations

Important vs Urgent

Another common problem on projects is that people do not prioritise the important tasks over urgent ones. This is particularly difficult when there is a powerful stakeholder who needs something that has not been prioritised by the project manager. We can all relate to the situation where our agenda or plan is thrown out by a request (or demand) from someone else.

As the project manager, it is your responsibility to make sure that this extra work is managed and managed well. There are few things more stressful for an employee than having multiple bosses, all with different urgent demands, and no one making decisions about what the priority order should be.

If your team are constantly Working On the Latest Fire (WOLF), they are not being effective. It's your job as an impactful project manager to make sure that they have the right structures and supports in place so that they can spend more of their time Easily Working Effectively (EWE). When you are doing 1:1s with your team members, one great question to ask is, 'Are you a WOLF or an EWE today?' If the answer is WOLF, you both have some work to do to sort out the situation.

Are you a WOLF or an EWE?

There are a few tricks you can use to make sure that your team are focused on important rather than urgent tasks.

Eisenhower Matrix

One of the most famous ways to figure out if your team are spending their time on urgent rather than important tasks is the Eisenhower matrix. It's a very simple four-section chart plotting urgency vs importance.

This is a traditional management tool and is covered in a lot of books, including the classic *"7 Habits of Highly Effective People"* by Stephen Covey. It was originally made famous by Dwight D Eisenhower and when you work through it, it sounds plausible.

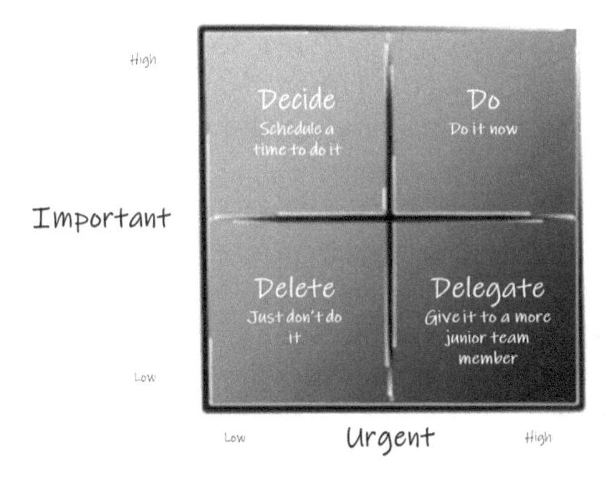

The Eisenhower matrix

The matrix states that you should spend your time on important, urgent things, schedule important non-urgent things, delegate unimportant urgent things, and delete everything that is not important or urgent. Seems sensible right?

I have no experience in the military, and I'm sure that in the life and death situations that Eisenhower was dealing with, this is a good way of quickly making decisions on how to prioritise things. However, I believe there are a few significant problems with this approach when it comes to normal business activity.

The main issue is that it leads to you delegating a load of urgent, not important tasks to your team members!

I have no idea why this strikes people as a good idea, or how it has snuck through the collective brains of hundreds of authors and millions of people. There is a fundamental point here that reduces the impact of a project manager – by delegating low-value tasks, people may be putting a high value on their own time, but they are putting a low value on their team's time! Ridiculous!

A much better version of the matrix emphasises importance much more. Instead of delegating urgent, low-value tasks, it should be the project manager's job to make sure that they are deleted as well! This might take a difficult conversation with a stakeholder or some degree of leadership, but surely it is better to explain to someone why a task is low value than to do it just because it is urgent!

During this conversation, you may find out that it is actually a high-value task, and you had misunderstood it. That's fine too as you can then treat it with the importance that it deserves. But to continue to consider something as low-value and simply palm it off on a more junior team member just to get it off your own plate is bad management and should be called out as such. Doing this will reward the perception that just because something is urgent, it should be done, even if it is not important. Be ruthless, be confident, and make sure both you and your team are only working on important tasks!

Picking apart this matrix further, I'd like to see that delegation happening much more often for important tasks. If, instead of doing a task yourself because it is important, you can delegate it to a team member wherever possible and coach and support them to be successful, then you will not only free up your own time, but you will also be building the skills of your team, helping them with their career, and motivating them to get better every day. You won't be able to delegate everything that's important, but if you do so wherever it is possible, you are not just completing the task but building capability for the future as well.

In another section of the matrix, Eisenhower has put that we should decide when we are going to do the non-urgent, important tasks. Again, I think the emphasis here is wrong. If you are genuinely working effectively and not firefighting all the time, you will spend almost all your time on Important, non-urgent tasks. This is a great place to be – you can be strategic, you can make good decisions, and you can improve the capabilities of your team. Rather than deciding when to do the things that are in this section, you should actively be trying to do them now, or even better, delegate them and coach your team to do them now.

I also prefer the term 'Diarise' instead of 'Decide' as it emphasises putting time into the diary to do the important, non-urgent task. This is a more proactive way of thinking about task management and is much more likely to end in the task being done.

I don't know how these things infiltrate popular culture, but perhaps there is a new version of the Eisenhower matrix that's required for the modern workplace. Maybe the 'Louttit Matrix' will gain some popularity as a term, and maybe it won't, but I'd like to hope that some people will spend a bit more time working on and delegating important tasks and a lot less time working on urgent unimportant ones!

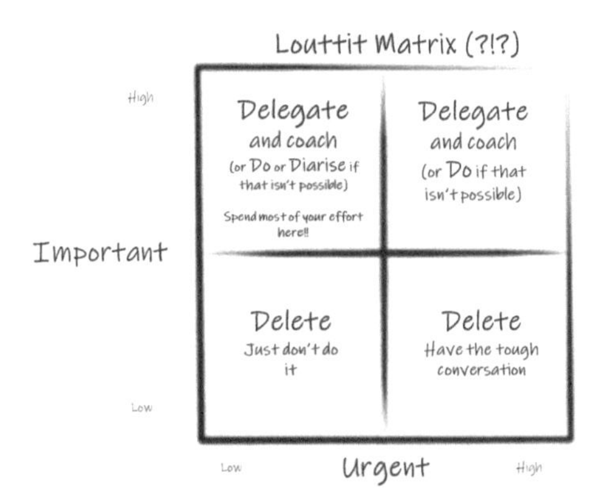

The Louttit matrix

It is a nice exercise to brainstorm the list of all the tasks that someone is working on and plot them on this matrix to get a sense of whether they are a WOLF or an EWE. I like to do this with Post-it notes (as you can imagine) and you can do it at an individual or team level. Once you have a sense of where people are spending their time, you can start to figure out how to move their work away from urgent and towards important.

I once led a team that were constantly firefighting. They would come into the office each day with great plans for what they were going to achieve, but within a couple of hours, they would be deep in some emergency that needed resolving ASAP. It quickly became clear to me that there were a couple of things I could do to help them move away from being WOLFs.

One of the biggest reasons the team were under so much pressure all the time was that what they were working on was not transparent and easily accessible to all their stakeholders. This meant that people got frustrated because they could not see the progress that was being made. It was made worse by the fact that they were right - because very little actual progress was being made.

I sat and discussed this with the team, and it became obvious that they were spending a lot of their time switching tasks and waiting for responses from business stakeholders. The stakeholders were happy to come along and bang their fists on the desk when they remembered that they'd asked for something and had some time, but they were not responding to my team's questions over email or attending the meetings where the work was being discussed. The fundamental problem was that the stakeholders were not valuing my team's time sufficiently highly in relation to the value and (intermittent) urgency they were putting on the work. To solve this problem, I used one of the great tools from Scrum – a sprint prioritisation session.

Prioritisation Meetings

Every two weeks, stakeholders who wanted something from the team had to turn up to the session which I chaired (refereed!) and negotiate amongst themselves what things my team would work on. Each item had a business value and an effort estimate, and we simply allocated the effort available in the next two weeks to the most important tasks as agreed in that meeting. If you didn't turn up to the meeting, if your requirements weren't thought through well, or if their business value wasn't clearly articulated, then your work simply would not get done!

The meeting would take all the work that was proposed for the next two weeks, add up the effort that it would take, and compare it to the capacity of the team. As the amount of work requested was invariably greater than the amount of effort available, there proceeded a negotiation, where stakeholders offered to push some of their requirements into a future sprint, or address part of the problem in a different way for a while to get their most important requirement into the current plan. In a positive, transparent process, where everyone understands how the decisions get made and everyone knows that they will have another chance in a couple of weeks, this can work beautifully.

The people with the most important work learned to use the system well. They minimised the asks on the IT team and made sure that they were extremely responsive to the team members whenever they needed anything.

We set up a regular training session in the diary every two weeks to explain the process to people so that they had no excuse to follow a different process and within a couple of months, we had trained all our stakeholders to turn up to that meeting when they wanted something done. We also emphasised the responsiveness of the stakeholder in the meeting. If my team were waiting on a response from someone, it became a talking point at that meeting – in front of their peers in the business. Suddenly, no one wanted to be called out for wasting the IT team's time because everyone could see how much work was needed and how busy the team were. Low-value work got canned because the stakeholders couldn't justify it to their peers, and everyone knew that they had to use the time they got from the IT team well.

Another benefit of this approach was that the 'fist banging' behaviour melted away over time. Whenever someone came along frustrated that their piece of work was not moving quickly enough, the team sent them to me and I took them for a coffee to explain the new way of working. If they wanted something done, there was a process in place for them to follow. They had to be ready to support their request and argue for its value in front of their peers, but if they did that, they would get what they needed.

If a piece of work wasn't included in this sprint, don't worry – we'll go through the whole thing again in two weeks – and if it's the most valuable thing for the company at that point, we'll do it then. If it's not, perhaps you should rethink what you are asking for or come up with a different solution than an IT fix.

In this way, we massively reduced the frivolous asks where we were expected to work on things that were only valuable to one or two people and were able to make improvements that generated real returns for the business at a much larger scale. We completed a lot more work and, more importantly, the work we completed was exponentially more valuable. I'd agreed a target with the CFO that we would complete €3 million worth of business value in my first year. When we added up all the projects we'd completed, it came in at over **€25 million** in business value (as estimated by the stakeholders who were asking for the work).

My whole team all got their full bonuses, and everyone switched from talking about how frustrated they were with the IT team to how great a job they were doing!

A Note on MoSCoW

Many other project management books propose a different way of prioritising work – one that I think is utterly out of date and causes more trouble than it solves. They propose that projects use the MoSCoW approach to prioritisation. This stands for:

- Must – Things that are critical for the project.
- Should – Not mandatory, but things that the customer really wants.
- Could – Things clients would like but can live without.
- Would – Things that the project probably won't do.

Essentially, what you do is take the whole list of requirements and allocate them to one of these four categories. I believe the only reasons why this approach has any credence whatsoever are that the acronym is kind of catchy and it was popularised during the 1980s when the Cold War was in the news, so it felt kind of newsworthy to Western audiences when it was introduced.

The problem with MoSCoW is that it anticipates a negotiation about the scope of the project without giving a way to decide between any two individual requirements (apart from at the edges of the categorisation groups).

Every time I have seen MoSCoW used in practice, the 'M' category has ended up massively over-scoped because the stakeholders rightly expect that anything that has a 'Should' rating will end up being descoped from the project by the end. They chuck in a few half-hearted 'Coulds' and 'Woulds' as cannon fodder for the upcoming scope prioritisation arguments and get ready to go into battle.

This dynamic destroys the whole purpose of prioritising the requirements in the first place and sets all the scoping discussions up for failure from the beginning.

Another disastrous flaw in MoSCoW is that it utterly fails to give any credit to a requirement for being easy to achieve. As no attempt is made to estimate the effort for each requirement, very hard things and very easy things are assumed to be equally worth doing, so the effort required to deliver the project often ends up being massively inflated by a few difficult requirements.

The final reason why MoSCoW is so bad is that it provides no way of distinguishing which requirement is more important than another within categories. It makes no attempt to determine whether one 'Must' requirement is better or worse than another 'Must' requirement, and so the discussion degenerates into a shouting match about all or nothing instead of a sensible discussion on which thing we should focus on first.

While MoSCoW feels like a good idea when you first hear about it, I would highly recommend that you plan to have a much more dynamic and flexible approach to scope. It is important to allow things to move up and down the priority list as our understanding of the project changes and only lock them in when you are about to do the actual work on them.

Managing Scope the Agile Way

So how should you manage scope when the world is changing and complex? The agile approach is to allow yourself to work with differently sized chunks of scope. You might identify five or six 'themes' for your project. Big areas of requirements that you know you are generally going to work on. Then you can prioritise these first. You might then break each of them down into several 'epics' or large requirements, which are then broken down further into 'user stories' and finally 'tasks'.

The key in agile is that you don't have to break all the themes, epics, or even user stories down immediately into tasks. Because you know that you are going to be constantly reviewing and improving your requirements, it's OK to work on one area in detail at the start of the project and trust yourselves to break down a less important area later in the project.

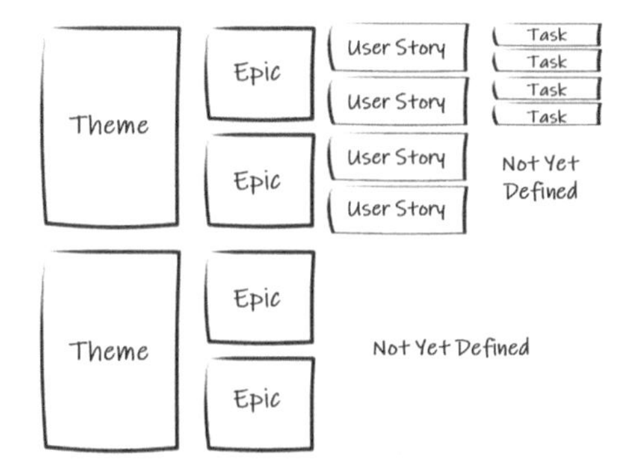

Agile scope management

Once you have some level of understanding of these requirements, you can put your best estimates of both value and effort against them (more on estimating later), and then create your 'work queue ' (also known as a 'Product Backlog'). This list will contain tasks, epics, themes, and user stories, all mixed up and prioritised so that the highest-value, lowest-effort ones are done first.

If your work queue has a theme or an epic at the top, you have some work to do to break that down into smaller chunks so that your team will have some high-value tasks to work on. If you have already done that, don't worry too much about what is coming down the line; just get on with the high-value work at the top of the work queue.

The beauty of this approach is that it allows you to work on getting value from the project early, even when there are a lot of unknowns around. Sometimes, you might need to include experiments or investigations into the work queue to help you figure out how to do some future work or make a big decision, but that's perfectly fine. When it's time to do those experiments and investigations, they will rise to the top of the work queue and get done!

Your work queue might look something like this (we'll explain more about how to come up with the numbers shortly):

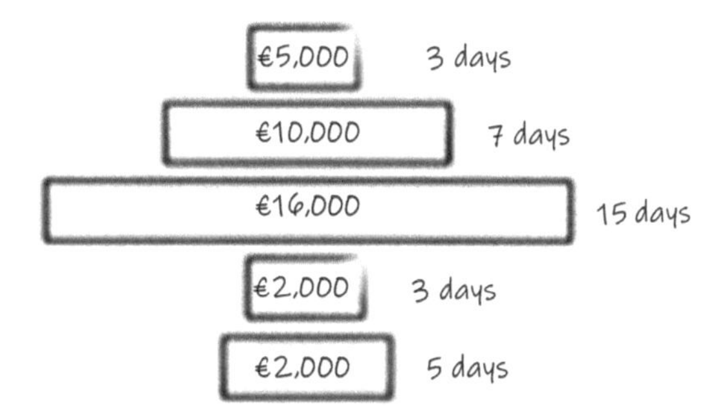

Work queue with value and effort

Note how the size of the task and its place in the queue are only part of the story. If you have a big one near the top, break it down into smaller chunks and get on with whatever is most important next.

To figure out the actual prioritisation, you need to estimate two things: value and effort.

Estimating Value

Value is one of the most important and hardest things to nail down. Some organisations will not even kick off a project until a detailed business case has been written, reviewed, challenged, argued about, left on a shelf for three months, and then eventually dusted off and approved.

The problem with a detailed business case is that it scares people away from writing it. They fear writing detailed business cases, because they know they will have to make assumptions that could turn out to be wrong. They are concerned that they may be held to account for delivering the business value that was approved, when the project's outcome is uncertain. That's why I like to make business cases much, much simpler and write them in just 30 minutes.

Creating a Basic Business Case

So how do you write a business case in 30 minutes? The following technique is what I taught to all the different people who wanted something from the IT team in Cpl. The training title was 'How to Articulate the Business Value of an IT Change' (Catchy – eh?). It was a session that I ran weekly, and where we started sending everyone who wanted something (significant) done by the IT team. By setting this 45-minute training session up, I gave my team a place to send all those fist-banging stakeholders when they wanted something that they felt was important. The session also gave me a way to funnel important stakeholders into a simple meeting where I could explain what we were trying to do in the IT team, why it was important, and how they could engage with our activities. The key steps to writing a simple business case are as follows:

1. Write down why you want to do the project in a single sentence.
2. Extract from that sentence the ways in which the project or change will impact the company's profits (insist on profits rather than revenue as even high-revenue projects can be unprofitable)
3. For each of these profit impacts, perform a simple calculation of how it will make more money for the company.

Expected Return = Value Added × Probability of Success

4. Add up the value of each of the different ways the project will increase the profits of the company and you have your business case.

Once your stakeholder has their business case written out, anyone can challenge any aspects of the total number. They might argue that the likelihood of success is lower or that the calculated expected return is too high. There is benefit in that challenge. The number will improve and become more credible with every conversation about it as you will find out different people's views of what the project would achieve. Your stakeholder can discuss this with colleagues and modify those calculations until they have a fair estimation of the business value that everyone can agree on. Once they have settled on a consensus for the business value, the business case can then be fed into the prioritisation discussion.

That's it for business value. You do the estimation of the effort required (see below) and work out where the task or project goes on the priority list.

It's useful to understand this process with an example.

Example 1 – The Basics

Statement

I want this report because it will save 5 people 3 hours per week each.

Business Value Calculation

5 People × 3 hours × €25 (average cost of an hour of work for these people) × 52 weeks × 3 years (3 years is a reasonable time horizon for these kinds of calculations) = €58,500

Likelihood of success

80% – We're quite confident we can save this time.

Overall risk-weighted Business Value

€58,500 × 80 % = €46,800 – round it down to €45,000 to reflect the fact that these numbers are all rough estimates, and we don't want to be accused of inflating the figures.

Here's the crucial bit

Now you discuss these assumptions with your stakeholders. Is €25/hour a reasonable weighted cost? Are all those people going to save 3 hours a week, or just some of them? Are we really 80% confident that the report will save the effort? Say you go through the estimates, and you figure out that the true value is more like:

4 People × 2.5 hours each × €30 per hour × 52 weeks × 3 years × 60% likelihood of full success = €28,080.

Round it down to €25,000 to be conservative and now you have a business case that both you and your stakeholder can agree on. You also have a set of assumptions that should stand up to scrutiny from other colleagues, but if they disagree with any of them, you can easily revise the calculation.

OK, I hear you ask: but what about the intangible benefits of a project, like making people happier, or reducing the risk of having a data breach? This is where the real skill comes in – you must assign a monetary value to those benefits, even though they are intangible. Doing this allows you to compare business value across all your team's demands and make great prioritisation decisions.

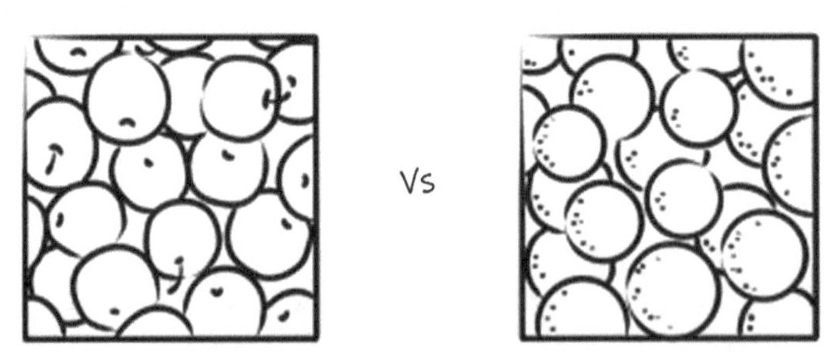

Don't compare apples to oranges

Example 2 – Intangible benefits

Example 1 was straightforward. Saving people's time is easy to calculate. So is additional profit per sale or being able to save a license fee. But what about the more intangible business cases like risk reduction or making customers happy? I would recommend that you hold yourself to the same process for these things as you do for the tangible benefits. You just use a higher level of uncertainty.

If another reason for building this report is that it will save a manual process that is prone to error and could result in a data breach, perhaps the calculation might go something like this:

Cost (including reputational damage) of a serious data breach = €1,500,000
Current likelihood of a serious data breach: 5% over 3 years
Likelihood of a data breach once we have built the report: 4.5% over 3 years.
Difference = 0.5%
Value of implementing the report = 0.5% × 1,500,000 = €7500

Again, you can then have the conversation with your stakeholders. Is the €1.5 million reasonable for the cost of a breach? Is this process so bad that it is really creating 10% of our risk (0.5% out of 5%) of having a data breach across the whole company? Will the risk be completely gone once the manual process is replaced? Etc.

I have done this calculation hundreds of times with different stakeholders. It never takes more than 30 minutes, and very often it takes just 10 minutes. Often, we realise that the business value is just so low that it's not worth doing – and for me, those are amongst the most important conversations I can have. In less than half an hour, I have significantly reduced the demands on my team, kept a stakeholder happy when they could have become really frustrated by being turned down, and learned some things about our business. A phenomenal use of my time.

As the organisation gets used to this approach and colleagues learn to write and review each other's business cases, you can drive a big increase in the value of work that you do. It also has the added benefit of allowing you to tell your boss (or The Board!) how much business value all those changes you are making add up to, according to the estimations of the people who are asking for the work in the first place.

The best things to work on are those that are high value and low effort. If you can relentlessly prioritise your to-do list by the highest-value, lowest-effort items, you will be working in the most effective way possible. So how do you figure out the other part of the calculation – the effort required?

Estimating Effort

Estimating the effort of a piece of work is easy. Getting it right can be very difficult! As a rule, the smaller or simpler the chunk of work that you are estimating, the closer you are likely to get to the actual amount of time and effort it will take. You will have to figure out the trade-off of spending time breaking things down into smaller chunks for management and estimation (micro-managing) vs saving that time by leaving the chunks quite large and accepting a higher level of risk that the estimates will be out by a bigger factor. The more experienced your team and the simpler the pieces of work, the larger you can leave the chunks and the less management they will require.

A great example of this is in the building trade. An experienced plasterer can walk into a room and, based on gut feel and historical experience, come up with an estimate of how long it will take her to prep and plaster the room and how much material she will need.

1. Get materials from van and set up: 20 minutes
2. Plasterboard the walls: 10 m^2 at 25 minutes per m^2 = 4 hours and 10 minutes
3. Plaster the walls: 10 m^2 at 20 minutes per m^2 = 3 hours 20 minutes
4. Tidy up and clean down: 20 minutes
   Total = 8 hours and 10 minutes

If I were estimating how long it will take me to plaster the same room (having never plastered one before), I should be including a lot more uncertainty in my estimates:

1. Watch a YouTube video on how to plaster a room (!): 1 hour
2. Buy the right supplies: 2 hours 30 minutes
3. Plasterboard the walls: 10 m^2 at 30 to 60 minutes per m^2 = 5 hours to 10 hours
4. Plaster the walls: 10 m^2 at 30 to 60 minutes per m^2 = 5 to 10 hours
5. Tidy up and clean down: 30 minutes
6. Redo any areas that I'm not happy with the following day: 2 to 4 hours
   Total: Somewhere between 15 and 28 hours

Estimating Simple or Repeated Work

Certain types of work, like building a house or installing an out-of-the-box piece of software, have been done many times before and have quite well-understood variables. In these cases, simply looking at what was done the last few times and taking an average can be a pretty good way to go. For example, the last time we installed this software on that type of server, it took two days, and this one appears to be very similar, so it's reasonable to assume that it will take two days this time with the same team – probably a bit less because we've done it before, so let's say 1.5 days.

Estimating Complicated Work

Estimating complicated – or poorly understood – work can be much trickier, and the consequences of getting it wrong are painful for everyone involved. If you over-estimate, you may find your team are not as productive as they could have been. You can also put people off from doing valuable things if they look too expensive or time-consuming. On the other hand, under-estimating work is damaging because it means that either you fail to meet the expectations that have been set, or your team ends up working long hours to meet the agreed timelines. None of this is great, but predicting the future is hard, so time spent on getting estimations as good as possible is rarely wasted. As a PM, it's going to be your job to guide the team into getting the best estimations they can in a reasonable time. Here are a few things to think about to help achieve this.

Planning Poker

There are lots of different ways that other books will tell you to use to estimate work: T-Shirt Sizes, Top-Down, Bottom-Up, Parametric, 3-point Estimating, etc. They all have their merits, but they miss a fundamental point: actually getting to a number of hours a task will take without just making it up on your own. My favourite estimation method by far avoids this problem by turning estimating into a structured conversation with all the knowledgeable people involved. It is from the world of agile, and it sounds like fun. Let me introduce you to Planning Poker.

This works at epic, story, and task levels. It's tricky with high-level themes but still works better than most other techniques. In Planning Poker, you gather the people who are most familiar with the project, technology, environment etc. in a room (or virtual room). You give them a set of Planning Poker cards, and someone describes the functional 'chunk' of work that needs to be done.

Planning poker

Once everyone in the group has a good idea of the work involved, they pick an estimate for the time that needs to be spent on the work from the set of Planning Poker cards based on the Avogadro series of numbers: 0, ½, 1, 2, 3, 5, 8, 13, 20, 50, 100.

Planning poker cards

We use this series of numbers as it gives a large range and highlights the fact that the larger the estimate, the more uncertain it is.

You can use hours, days, or even person weeks as the relevant unit for the discussion, depending on whether you are estimating small things (tasks) or big things (epics).

Once everyone has revealed their cards, you will see that either everyone agrees or there is some disagreement in the group. This is where the magic happens! The team members then discuss why they have voted for their number. 'I think the number is big because we have to clean the data before we extract it' or 'I think it's small because I have found a great piece of software that can do this thing for us already.' The team discuss all these points and then vote again. The discussion allows people to fill in gaps in each other's knowledge and should enable them to come to a consensus on the most realistic estimate. After two or three rounds, the team should have a good idea of both the estimate of the work and how they are going to go about it.

The hardcore agile teams use a thing called "story points" instead of hours to estimate how much work they can fit into a sprint. There is a good theory behind story points, and I'm sure that they work well in pure software development teams; however, they have one major flaw – no one else understands them!

Because they are, by definition, related to the speed and experience of the team, and different teams will be able to get through different numbers of story points in a sprint, I have found that they tend to confuse anyone outside of the team (and very often those within the team as well)! For this reason, after three separate failed attempts on different projects to get stakeholder groups to understand how story points work, I have now officially given up, and I recommend that people simply use hours or days for their estimates.

If you and your team think story points are a great idea, please do go ahead and use them; in many ways they are better for estimating than just using hours or days. But my advice would be to think carefully about how you explain these estimates to people outside your team. And if you have figured out a brilliant way to explain them to stakeholders outside of the team, I'd love to hear about it.

My LinkedIn Profile is:

https://www.linkedin.com/in/james-louttit/

(If you'd like to hear about other PM and leadership concepts and/or share your own, it would be great to connect.)

Break Things into the Right-Sized Chunks – Goldilocks Estimating

Some tasks are hard to estimate because they are just too big. They are intimidating and hard to get your head around. With big tasks like these, it's important to break them down. Archbishop Emeritus Desmond Tutu once described 'How to eat an elephant', and his solution is very applicable to projects and estimating. His answer, 'one bite at a time', is crucial if you are going to avoid analysis paralysis and make progress on your project.

How to eat an elephant – one bite at a time

Estimating something that is going to take a team of people three weeks to do is fraught with risk. Your chances of getting your estimate close to the real-world result are quite slim at this high level. Pieces of work this size are complex and have lots of elements. Likewise, if you are breaking down your tasks into things that are going to take only a few minutes, you are at too detailed a level for your estimation, and you'll end up micro-managing the whole thing and spending more time tracking tiny tasks than getting anything done. This is why I like to recommend that you use differently sized chunks, depending on how close the piece of work is to actually starting

Break it into the right sized chunks

It's handy to have a base idea early on of how much effort each of the big chunks is going to take in the project. Breaking up the project into, say, 10 'themes' is a great way to get something down on paper for everything that you are aware of. As you progress through the project, you might pick a 'theme' to work on and break that down into 'epic' stories that are still really big, but a bit better understood. The next step is to break the 'epics' down into 'stories' and finally into 'tasks'.

Then you provide a range on the estimates that reflects the level of effort and detail that has gone into estimating it. Themes have a big range, epics a smaller one and, by the time you are estimating tasks, you should have a tight range.

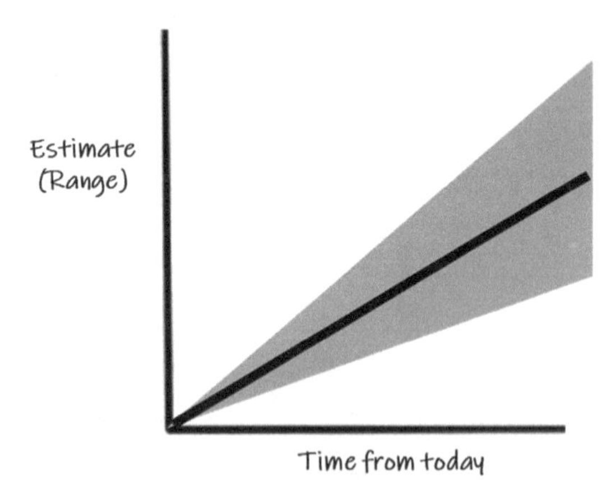

The further away the estimate is, the bigger the uncertainty

In this way, you can make progress through the project on the most valuable and easiest themes – without having to estimate everything at a detailed level before you know much about it. This approach also allows you to make good decisions about what to work on next while leaving it clear to stakeholders that there is uncertainty around the estimates into the future.

Weighing Up Value and Effort

Now you can see how you can come to your prioritised work queue. For each piece of work, you have an idea of the business value and the effort it's going to take. If you want to be formal about it, you can divide a task's value by its effort and prioritise the work that will give you the most value per hour worked. Some things may have to wait until later in the project for other reasons (you can't build a roof until after you've built the walls), but you can use the value and effort numbers you now have to force proper prioritisation and develop the all-important work queue we talked about earlier. Here is that work queue again, but now you should know how to fill in the numbers.

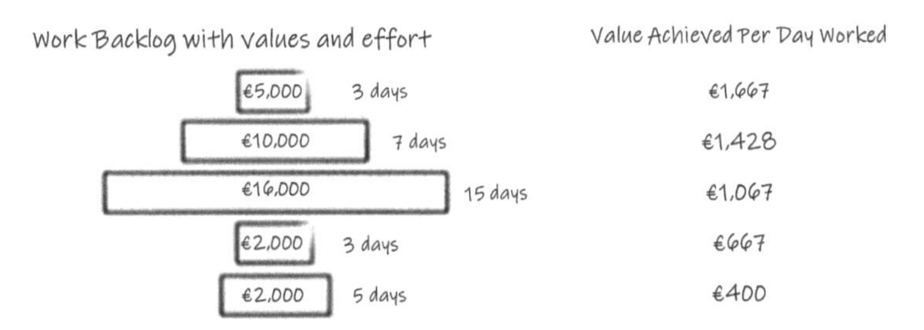

Work queue with value and effort

You can see that it is the combination of value and effort that is pushing things to the top. Small, high-value tasks first, followed by larger, high-value tasks. The lower-value tasks appear further down the list.

Some people like to put the actual "value per day worked" calculations explicitly in their work queue so that they can actively keep that focus on high value/low effort work. I think this is useful, as long as the nuances of the discussion are not boiled down to "just" a number. Often other considerations, such as a regulatory deadline, or the need to build walls before you build roofs will drive the timeframe and ordering of your tasks alongside this calculation.

Trim the Tail

If you have done a great job of figuring out your prioritisation and working on high-value, low-effort items, and you've been progressing your project for a while, the work on the queue starts to become both harder and less valuable.

When you are starting to build a product, there should be lots of easy things that you can do to make it better, but once you have an established product, it becomes harder and harder to improve. A lot of products reach this point, but they have a team of people working on them, and they still have some customers who have asked for things, so the team just keeps working through the list. This can be quite a wasteful situation in which to operate. While adding a feature that will definitely be used and loved by 100% of customers every day is a great way to spend your time, adding a feature that might be used by 0.1% of customers once a year probably isn't. There is a temptation in many stakeholders to ask for things that do not add much value because they do add *some* value. This is where your prioritisation processes are crucial.

There is a phrase used by the Scrum community called 'trimming the tail', which is a useful concept here. As an impactful project manager, you should be on the lookout for the point where the cost of adding another feature is greater than the value that the feature will bring. That should be the end of the project!

In fact, it's a bit earlier than that. If there are other projects where your resources could be used to add more value for the same effort, there should be a discussion about shifting resources (usually people) to a new project where there are better value-adding opportunities.

Of course, if you are working hard at coming up with great ideas for features, you may be able to come up with some that are high value and low effort even late in the project, but impactful project managers look for opportunities to trim the tail whenever appropriate and move on to something else.

Visualise and Communicate

Once you have your priorities clear, visualising and communicating them is a key part of the project manager's job. Whether you use a Kanban board, a status report, a prioritisation meeting, or some other mechanism, it's crucial that stakeholders can see the priorities that your team are working on. If you have your project plan or prioritised Kanban board on your computer and just manage it yourself, you are working on what I like to call an 'information refrigerator'.

Information refrigerators

You are keeping that information to yourself and people have to come to you to find out what is going on. If you do this, a lot of your time will be unnecessarily spent on answering questions about what your team are working on and when they will get to something else.

Instead, you should publish the information on an 'information radiator'. Then people can simply keep themselves up to date with what is going on as much as they want or need to. You are free to use your time much more effectively for managing risks, negotiating with stakeholders, or coaching your team, all of which will stand your project in a much better place than answering simple questions that could have been easily resolved just by making information more easily available.

Information radiators

Information radiators also create opportunities for you to occasionally get a serendipitous bit of bonus help. If someone sees one of your risks and has an idea on how to mitigate it or notices on your radiator that you have a dependency they can help with, you might just get lucky and save a lot of time and effort.

Another benefit of information radiators comes when a stakeholder hasn't been paying enough attention to your project. If you have been tracking a specific risk to the project in your private risk log, and that risk then comes to pass, your stakeholders may be annoyed at you for not telling them that this might happen. If, however, you have been including that risk in your weekly status report, they can't really complain that they didn't know as it is their job to read your status report (whether they do so or not is up to them). This means they can't really be upset about finding something out late because you got the information to them in good time. The only thing they can reasonably do is help you resolve the issue. It's a subtle but powerful way of getting implicit support for your project from people who are too busy to read your status report. At least you sent it them!

Some great information radiators include:

- Kanban boards
- Status reports
- Company/CEO updates
- Newsletters
- Project management tools like Jira or Monday.com on a screen in the office, with full team access for real-time updates
- The company's internal website home page
- The desktops on people's computers (these can be updated with regular push notification messages by the central IT team nowadays)

Retrospectives and Estimating

Unfortunately for most organisations, it is quite rare to look back on your estimates once a piece of work is completed. If you want to continuously improve your estimates, it is well worth taking a bit of time to do this. Did you and your team massively over- or under-estimate compared to the reality of what happened? Did you get lucky or unlucky? Should you have identified more risks that would have allowed you to include more contingency, or did you get it about right? The key here is not to blame your past selves for making a mistake with the estimates. It's about helping your future selves to learn and hopefully get your estimates closer to reality in the future.

With these tools, you should be in a better place to manage your project's scope, but what about the things that could go wrong? Risks, and their associated partners' assumptions, dependencies, and issues are another set of powerful tools that impactful project managers use when steering their projects to success.

Chapter 6
Risks (and Assumptions, Dependencies, and Issues) – Managing What Could Go Wrong

Managing risks – are you going to need a bigger boat?

Before we get onto the key topic of risks, it is worth talking about their little brothers, assumptions. Assumptions are innocuous thoughts that we all have about what is going on in the project. They are very often hidden away in our brains and not even discussed with other people, but assumptions can grow – sometimes very quickly – into risks, dependencies, and issues.

Assumptions

Many projects come unstuck because the idea one person has about what is going to happen is different from that of another person. This is fine at the beginning of a workshop, or very early in a project, if it is resolved and everyone gets onto the same page, but if the ambiguity or misunderstanding lasts too long, it can cause huge problems later.

Inexperienced project managers often look around the room at the beginning of a project and see things through rose-tinted spectacles. They see all the other nice people and they work on the basis that everyone else knows the same things they do. They firmly believe that everyone is on the same page.

https://doi.org/10.1515/9783111271149-006

Getting everyone on the same page

In reality though, you will often find there are a lot of people who are not on the same page. Sometimes, they're not even in the same book! People's implicit understanding of various situations can be very different from one another and can change quite dramatically over time.

Realising everyone isn't on the same page

One of the best ways to make sure that everyone is on the same page about what the project is doing is to write down and share the assumptions that you are working under. This has several advantages.

- Written assumptions make you really think about the different angles that the project needs to deal with and tighten up your own understanding of them.
- Written assumptions can be shared with people and can force them to voice their concerns about misalignment.

- Written assumptions give you a place to stand later in the project, when a stakeholder who wasn't paying attention becomes unhappy that something didn't go the way that they were expecting it to. (This can happen a lot if you are not careful!)

The kinds of assumptions that you might write down at the start of the project include:

- It is assumed that the project team will work together in the office one day per week.
- It is assumed that sign-offs will be received from key stakeholders within 5 working days.
- It is assumed that XXX (key person) will be allocated to the project for 2.5 days per week.

By writing these things down, the goal is to force colleagues to either agree with the assumption or share their concerns nice and early. You are using them to clarify the parameters of the project and reduce the likelihood of nasty surprises later on.

The Lifecycle of an Assumption

Assumptions are so powerful because they allow you to table your concerns without blaming anybody. If they are handled well, they can help you get off to a great start. If you call out an assumption, tell all the stakeholders, and everyone agrees to it, you can be comfortable that it's valid, and you can move on with the project. Leave it in the minutes or the RAID log (Risk, Assumption, Issue, Dependency) and keep an eye on it in case it grows into something more concerning. Pat yourself on the back for calling it out and sleep well in the knowledge that you have it covered in case you need to come back to it in the future.

Writing an assumption is the start of a process. Some assumptions are quite benign. They sit there in the RAID log all the way through a project, getting checked and validated occasionally, but generally do nothing other than provide a foundation for everyone's understanding of the project and keep stakeholders on the same page. Some assumptions, however, tend to have a habit of growing into bigger, more pressing things for a project manager to be aware of.

The quality of your assumptions and how you manage them lays the groundwork for your dependency, risk, and issue management throughout the project. If you manage your assumptions well, you'll be in a good place to deal with risks and issues. If you don't put the effort into setting your assumptions, you'll suffer later when they grow into dependencies, risks, and issues.

Assumptions

Assumptions can become risks and dependencies.

Assumptions, risks and dependencies

Risks and dependencies can become worse over time.

Risks and dependencies need managing

They can eventually turn into issues that threaten your whole project.

By the time it's an issue, it's too late

The lifecycle of an assumption.

Lifecycle of an assumption

Risks

I once worked in a large bank, where there was a strong culture of risk management. Unfortunately for those of us managing projects, the risk management culture was all about operational risk rather than project risk. This led to lots of confusion as the ways that you manage operational risk are quite different from the ways that you manage project risk.

- **Operational risks** are general risks to your business. For example, the risk that an employee might hurt themselves or that there might be a security breach and your data could be stolen.

- **Project risks** are risks to the goals of your specific project – for example, that you might not get support from the right people, or that the contract with a supplier may not get signed in time for the first phase of the project to start.

As a project manager, it's important that you understand the difference between these two types of risk. You are 100% responsible for **project risks** but, unless your project is set up to specifically address an **operational risk,** you need to make sure all the operational risks are being managed elsewhere. If your project is set up to deal with some operational risks, you treat these as scope, as work that needs to be done. You then need to work with the rest of the management team to ensure that they are resolved as part of your project.

Distinguishing between operational risk and project risk is crucial because, at some point, by definition, your project is going to end. Operational risks are ongoing risks that need to be managed by the business. If you find yourself owning them after the project is complete, you have moved from project management to just plain management. Maybe that's a career move you want to make, but I recommend that you make an active choice to do that rather than just allowing yourself to end up with a load of operational risks as part of your project.

Managing Risks

Risks are tricky things to manage because, by definition, they haven't happened yet. You need to figure out how much effort you should put into managing which risks. There are two considerations for every risk, which you can use to prioritise where you spend your time: probability and impact.

High-Probability, Low-Impact Risks

Some risks are high probability and low impact; for example, the risk that one of your team members will catch a cold and have to take a few days off. It's almost guaranteed that this will happen over the course of the project and, apart from asking people to wash their hands, there's not much you can do to stop it. These are things that you just manage in the day-to-day management of the project and don't spend a lot of time worrying about in advance.

Low-Probability, High-Impact Risks

Some risks work the other way around. They are low probability and high impact, e.g., the risk that the building burns down. If this happened, it could be a disaster for your project, but there are fire alarms and sprinkler systems and not many buildings burn down nowadays, so again, this is not an area to spend much of your time and effort.

High-Probability, High-Impact Risks

This is the area of risk management where you get the most return for your effort. Identifying the risks that are both high probability and high impact and doing something to prevent them from coming to pass is one of a project manager's most important jobs. A high-probability, high-impact risk might be something like a vendor dispute that could soon be reaching crisis point, where one of your suppliers is going to stop working on the project. If they stop work, the project could be set back a long way or might even need to be cancelled. Putting time and effort into resolving this vendor dispute might become the most important thing you do as a project manager this week.

Probability and Impact Can Change Over Time

The reason we note down risks and manage them using probability and impact is that these parameters can change over time. Maybe the vendor dispute developed from a small oversight of someone not paying a bill, or it could be a disagreement about scope. The risk that someone gets ill on the project could be small and not require action until the point where a global pandemic hits and suddenly you need to ask everyone to work from home for two years to avoid the whole project team becoming ill at the same time. Keeping track of your risks and actively managing the high-probability, high-impact ones each week will help you avoid the worst thing that the assumption gremlin can turn into: an issue.

Dependencies

Assumptions can also turn into dependencies. These are a bit like risks in that they can derail your project if they are not well managed. That said, the key to understanding dependencies is that they are not in your control. Dependencies are where a project manager's negotiating and stakeholder management skills can really be put to the test. This is where influencing other projects or stakeholders to take your priorities seriously is critically important. Sometimes, your dependencies become risks and issues. Other times, they simply disappear as other scheduled work outside of your project gets completed. Either way, they are something you need to keep a close eye on to make sure that they don't prevent you from achieving your project's goals.

Managing Dependencies

Dependencies are things that the project manager doesn't have direct control over, but that are still required for completion of part of the project. They are one of the most overlooked elements of project management, and one of the biggest causes of project delays. The easiest thing to do with a dependency is to hope that the person responsible for it completes their work in the timeframe that you need. That's also the worst thing to do with dependencies!

If you are going to be an impactful project manager, then it's the outcomes of the project that are going to be important to you, not the ability to blame someone else when things go wrong. Weak project managers just call out the dependency and get on with resolving things that are in their control. Impactful project managers find out ways of ensuring that the thing they are dependent on gets done when they need it done.

To illustrate this, I'll give an example from a project I was running a few years ago. As part of the project, we needed to put privileged user access monitoring (PUAM) in place on our new system. I won't get too technical, but this is basically a security feature where people who have high levels of access to the system have monitoring on their accounts in case they make a mistake or try to steal data or money. Only one of my stakeholders cared about PUAM, but she was an important one who could prevent the project from going live if she wasn't happy with the IT security.

Alongside my project, there was another project running, which was building an overall PUAM solution for the whole organisation. They were due to finish several months before my project, so we should have been able to just switch on their solution with our system. This was a classic dependency – something we needed that someone else was doing – so I called it out on the dependency log and carried on with my project. However, as an impactful project manager, I also took the PUAM project's manager for a coffee to find out how he was getting on. What I heard was not great. They didn't really have a solution and there was a lot of work to be done. Still, we had plenty of time and he had a plan, so it didn't feel like a big risk. I made a note to keep an eye on this dependency.

We had several other dependencies called out which turned out fine without any intervention, but a few weeks later, I reached out to the PUAM manager to see how they were getting on. They hadn't made much progress and, even though the date they were publishing for the go-live was still well within my project's needs, I decided it was time to flag this to my stakeholders. I called the PUAM dependency out as one of my top-three discussion points at the steering meeting. My stakeholders were mostly trading and finance people who did not care one bit about PUAM, so I kept it brief. I explained what PUAM was and why we needed it, and that I was going to keep a close eye on that project.

As we progressed over the next few months, I kept track of the PUAM project, and I upgraded it from a dependency to a risk to my project when it started to look like it wasn't going to be ready in time. My project was much bigger than the PUAM one and had a lot more resources behind it, so me flagging this risk got some senior people worried about it as well. As the likelihood of our project being affected by the delays in the PUAM project grew from low through medium to high over a period of weeks, it eventually became our project's biggest risk. At this point, I went to the overall head of project delivery and requested that we roll the PUAM project into my project and put more resources into it. I was able to bring in a very experienced and impactful senior manager to take over the PUAM project and push it forwards with the full weight of my much-bigger project.

We quite quickly got under the bonnet of the PUAM project and changed the scope to take out some of the things that we didn't need and that the original team had been finding difficult to deliver. After this, we made enough progress so that, while the PUAM project delays did impact our timelines, it only pushed us back by about a week, which everyone was happy with.

The key to this story is the stakeholder journey that we took our steering group on. From hearing about PUAM for the first time in March, they were able to get behind putting a lot more resources into solving an issue that had nothing to do with their business needs by September. This senior group were happy to put in the extra resources because the system we were building would be so transformational for their business that the extra cost was well worth spending.

Impactful project managers don't assume that other people will complete their dependencies on time. They keep an eye on them and look for opportunities to de-risk and help the other projects wherever possible. Your sphere of influence is large, and if you are good at engaging with your stakeholders, you can head off these kinds of potential disasters with timely action and good communication.

Issues

Another distinction that is sometimes difficult to articulate is the difference between a risk and an issue. My favourite way of thinking about this one goes like this:

> *"If you can smell it, it's a risk. If you are standing in it, it's an issue."*

The two things are managed differently, so make sure you know which one you are talking about.

Risk management

Issue management

Managing Issues

Issues need a different approach to risks and dependencies. While it's often OK to keep a watching brief on risks and dependencies and just give a nudge here and there to keep things on track, issues are directly impacting your project right now. If you've done a good job of risk and dependency management, you'll hopefully be able to avoid too many issues, but they will still happen to even the best-run projects. When issues occur, the question becomes how to deal with them.

When a new issue arises, you have to strike a balance between getting the news out there and making sure that people feel confident that you are able to manage it. As a rule, you have only a short amount of time to make a plan when a major issue hits, before the focus shifts to communicating with stakeholders and making sure that you demonstrate how you are managing it. As one of my early mentors explained to me when I came across my first major project issue, "bad news does not get better with age."

Bad news does not get better with age

Some issues are easy to fix, and a quick chat with a stakeholder can resolve them once you are aware of the problem. Others take more effort. Interestingly, just like scope items, there is no consistent relation between the impact of the issue (the value of resolving it) and the effort required to resolve it. Just because something is high impact does not mean that it is hard to resolve. Crisis management needs to happen when an issue is both important and urgent.

We've all heard the story of the boy who cried wolf. The basic premise is that the boy asked for help repeatedly and with high levels of urgency. The story goes that when he really needed help, none came. As a project manager, you must be very careful of your approach to putting urgency into a situation, particularly when you are asking for something that is not right at the core of what your stakeholder wants to achieve. Urgency is something that people like to see in others but do not like to have imposed on themselves, so it's something you need to spend carefully.

I was once on a training course where we were given the task of presenting a proposal for some new project resources to a senior stakeholder. The course's organisers were taking this seriously. They had brought in retired C-level executives from large companies to act as the executives in the role-play, and we were expecting to be grilled on our proposals.

My training group and I had spent the whole morning putting together a detailed slide deck with the proposal, thinking about the value proposition, how we were going to make it easy for the senior stakeholder to say yes to our proposal, who would present which bits of the plan etc. With 15 minutes to go before the meeting was due to take place, one of the course trainers dropped an innocuous-looking piece of paper onto our table. It was an email from someone in our project team, saying there was an issue with the client's website (which was managed by a different team in our consulting company). Not our responsibility, but well worth being aware of ahead of this meeting. Great to get the heads-up.

All the other training groups read this email and carried on with the preparation for the presentation. Some of them added a slide at the beginning of the deck referring to the issue and asked for even more money and resources to help make sure that this kind of thing got resolved quickly. I was lucky, though. I'd been in this kind of situation before, and I knew exactly what to do.

I quickly grabbed a flip chart, scrawled a picture of some servers and databases with some lines between them onto it (this was a training course, so I had to make it up), and wrote down some actions that seemed like they would be good actions to take in responding to the issue with the client's website:

- We think the issue is to do with a stack overflow in DB 11.
- We have a plan to resolve it.
- We need your sign-off to take the website down for 15 minutes and re-boot the servers.

As the meeting started, we did a small bit of theatre. Everyone else walked into the room, ready with the pre-prepared presentation for the meeting that was in the diary. As they were getting into their seats, I dashed into the room with the flip chart in hand, apologised for taking up the first part of the meeting, and explained the urgency of the website situation. I then explained how we were going to resolve it and what I needed from the executive. After getting what I needed, I made a big show of dashing back out of the room with the sign-off for the outage and rushing down the corridor to resolve the issue. This left the rest of my project team to have the original meeting that had been planned, present their proposals and win the business.

You can imagine what happened in every other room on the training course. The consultants were soundly lambasted for asking for more money and resources when our company was so clearly doing a bad job of running the website. None of the other teams won the deal, but we did!

This is what I mean by the 'right level of urgency'. If you are a great project manager, you will know your stakeholders well enough to understand how urgent and important each thing is to them, and you will act (and I do mean *act!*) in a way that reflects the level of energy that they want from you and your team. If you get it right, you have a much better chance of getting them to help you with what you need, when you need it!

The Theatre of a Crisis

There are times when you are dealing with an urgent issue, when the performance of how you are dealing with it really matters. Even if you and the team are working very hard on resolving an urgent issue, people can get very frustrated if they can't see that work. This is especially true if the issue is impacting customers or clients who are calling in and complaining. There are a few things that you can do to take the sting out of this situation.

- **Make sure that the key stakeholders who care about the issue are in your corner and working on whatever they can do to help.** Even if it's getting coffees and doughnuts for the team members who are fixing the issue, getting these people involved will keep them on the 'inside' of the problem rather than on the 'outside', ready to criticise whatever you are doing.
- **Demonstrate urgency with a 'war room'.** Even the name says what's going on. This can be an office space where the team gather to fix the problem (in which case, a sign on the door saying 'War Room' will demonstrate the urgency.) Another great way to create a war room is to have a virtual meeting that everyone can dial into at any time to get an update. As the PM, you should stay dialled into that call as much as possible. That way, people can find you and ask you how it's going or whether they can help.
- **In a crisis, you need more status reports, not fewer!** I've seen project managers who get into a crisis on the project cancel status and steering meetings. This is one of the worst things that you can do. While it might feel like keeping people updated with what's going on is less important than fixing the issue, in reality, it becomes even more important!

Demonstrating urgency – the war room

Increasing the frequency of status reports and reducing the level of detail down to just the immediate crisis can be a powerful way of showing action. The shortest frequency I've ever had for updates was about every two hours. This gives some time for the situation to develop but shows how seriously everyone is taking the issue. It's a good idea to sign off this kind of update with something like, 'The next update will be at 14:30, after our call with the vendor.' This keeps people off your back for a little while to allow you to concentrate on the problem you're working on. If you make a promise for an update at 14:30, though, you need to make sure that it happens at 14:30. You can quickly lose people's trust that you have the situation in hand if you don't.

- **Think hard about what you are communicating and how.**
  - Be transparent.
  - Be clear about what you do and don't know.
  - Deal in facts, not speculation that could turn out to be untrue.
  - Tell people what actions are underway and, unless they are really, genuinely helping, keep them away from the team members who are working to resolve the issue.
  - Keep a record of what was done and when. This can be useful learning lessons once the dust has settled.
- **Avoid blaming people and stop people from blaming each other.** It does not help the situation. Even the best project managers sometimes find themselves managing a crisis. It is a great time to show off just how great you are as a project manager. How you deal with it matters a lot more than how you got there.

Hopefully, this has given you a flavour of what assumptions, dependencies, risks, and issues are and how to manage them. Now the skill will be in making sure that you give this part of your job the right amount of airtime with your stakeholders.

How Many to Talk About – The Rule of 3

OK great. You've documented a load of risks, assumptions, issues, and dependencies (RAID items). You're covered! No one can accuse you of not being a diligent project manager. If you have documented 47 RAID items, covered all the bases, and captured them in a place where the stakeholders can see them, you should be OK when they start becoming problems later, right?

Wrong!

This is where the skill of being a project manager really kicks in, and the great PMs start to distinguish themselves from those that are simply following the formula. You are a project manager, and your main job is to deal with people, real people. As the economics profession discovered after the financial crisis in the late 2000s, people are not the rational, easy-to-predict, value-seeking geniuses of historical economic models. People are real people. They are busy, they make mistakes, they get distracted, they have many priorities that do not align with yours, they forget things, and, worst of all, they don't know everything that you know.

What this means for your well-thought-out RAID management approach is that you need to treat people like people. This means accepting the fact that they are not going to read, digest, respond to, and help you manage every single one of your 47 RAID items. If you have done all the things you need to do to build a great relationship with them, they might – if you are really lucky – help you with one or two things a week if those things aren't either their direct responsibility or delegated to them by their manager.

For the project team, this isn't a problem. You are assigning their work, so if you think something is important, you can work with them to make sure it happens. For everyone else, this is a huge challenge. The success of your project can easily depend on that apparently grumpy, stressed-out member of the steering committee. The one who didn't really want the company to do this project in the first place and who is fighting for resources to give to other projects.

So how can you make sure that your list of 48 RAID items (not a typo, you just thought of another one!) is taken seriously? The answer is to prioritise them. You need that detail. You need the 48 RAID items so that you can keep an eye on them and see how they develop (if at all). And you need to keep your RAID log in a transparent place, where it is available to everyone, and ensure that the key people have been asked to read (and possibly sign off) on it. However, you must not make the mistake of expecting everyone else to take the RAID log as seriously as you or be as diligent as you are going to be in managing it. That's why I recommend the 'rule of 3' for managing assumptions, dependencies, risks, and issues. Whenever you need to discuss any RAID items with any stakeholder or group of stakeholders, you should have a top 3 – and only three! These should be:

1. **I need help with this today.** I'm raising this item and giving you an action to help me resolve it.
2. **This is coming down the line.** I'll probably need some help with this item soon, or now, if it's easy for you to help me with it.
3. **Something to be aware of that could become urgent in the future.**

Your list of three things can be different for each stakeholder or each stakeholder group, and all of them should be called out on your bigger list of 49 items (damn it!). Realistically, though, your stakeholder (or stakeholder group) will only be able to help you with one thing, so make sure you pick the one that's going to have the biggest impact and give it the appropriate level of urgency. If you start talking about numbers 4, 5, and 6 on the list, stakeholders will lose interest and start to wonder why they employed you as the project manager. They will also get distracted from helping you with your number 1 RAID item, the one that you most urgently need them to help you with. So, keep it to three things (they can be risks, issues, dependencies, or assumptions), and make sure that you make it as easy as possible for stakeholders to help you in the ways that you and the rest of the project team cannot do for yourselves.

Chapter 7
Time – How to Predict the Future

People think project managers have a crystal ball to tell the future

One of the most frequently asked questions you'll get as a project manager is, 'When will it be finished?' It's your job to have an answer to that question but also to make sure that any changes to the schedule are managed and communicated so well that everyone is happy with them and feels in control. As I mentioned before, there is a risk of 'crystal bullshit' with all predictions of the future, but if you are managing risks, decisions, and communication well, you have a good chance of taking your stakeholders on the journey with you. By giving people choices between scope, cost, and time at every juncture, you should be able to make it clear to the important stakeholders that it's their decisions that drive the timeline, and that they can keep to the schedule if they decide that is important.

Risks and Time

When I first started out in project management, I was told that 80% of projects fail. This didn't sound like a great place to start, so I have kept careful track of all my projects since. There have been occasions where projects I managed were canned due to external factors or went in a different direction than originally thought, many times taking longer and costing more as a result. Still, I feel confident in saying that, at least in the second half of my project management career, none of them failed. To me, a failed project is one where the stakeholders are disappointed in the end.

They could be disappointed because they didn't get what they needed, the costs got out of control, or the project took longer than they'd expected. However, it's important to make sure that you are held to account for what the stakeholders want at the project's end – not what they thought they'd wanted at its start. I'll talk about

https://doi.org/10.1515/9783111271149-007

decisions a lot more in the chapter on stakeholders, but for now, it's worth noting that if you give your stakeholders control over the project's decisions, you are much more likely to have happy (or at least supportive!) stakeholders at the end.

Allowing people to make decisions means being proactive about those RAID items we talked about in the previous chapter.

If your risks are managed well, you will be communicating with your stakeholders about them from the moment they start to emerge. While you must be selective about how many you draw attention to at any given point, each risk to the scope, timeline, or cost in the project needs either an implicit or explicit decision from your key stakeholders. Most of the time, these will be 'wait and see' type implicit decisions, perhaps with some small mitigating actions. However, for risks, issues, and dependencies that will impact something important, you need to force an explicit decision and make sure that everyone's hands are just as dirty as yours on the route that is chosen.

As the PM, your job will be to present options with the consequences of each option clearly thought out. You can give a recommendation, but it is imperative that the stakeholders most affected by a decision are included in making it, and that they are brought onto the same page at the time the decision is to be made. If they are not, then you will start to see them falling away as supporters of the project, and they will start sniping from the side-lines. If people feel like they have been steamrollered, their views have not been taken into consideration, or they have a better way of doing things, you are losing them as positive stakeholders to the project, and this is one of the biggest risks to having a successful outcome for everyone.

You'll never be able to prove that a different approach would have had more issues than the one that was chosen, so the time when you need to get everyone behind you is the decision point. They should all agree with the approach and be on the record as having supported it. That's difficult, and we'll talk more about how to make it happen in the chapter on stakeholders, but it is an important goal for the project manager to keep detractors of the project to the absolute minimum possible.

Thinking about how you manage risks and communication applies most strongly to the 'Time' lens because timing is where the impacts of things going wrong will be most keenly noticed by your stakeholders. Missing planned milestones is the most likely reason why people will complain about a project that is struggling. If you can change the conversation from 'we missed the milestone because . . .' to 'we decided to push out the milestone because . . .', you will have a much better chance of being considered a good project manager in the end.

If you are running a traditional waterfall project, the 'plan' or timeline is something that will be heavily scrutinised whichever way you present it (usually through a Gantt chart – more below). However, if you are running an agile project, the discussion is much more about the scope of the next sprint, so the overall timeline can become less clear. This is why agile projects use something called a 'burndown' chart to explain how quickly we are getting through the work and when we think we'll be finished.

Communicating the Plan in Agile Projects – Burndown Charts

However good a job you have done of explaining agile to your stakeholders, they are still going to want to know when certain things are going to be completed. To do this, you can use your product queue and a thing called 'team velocity' to work out when things will be done. Let's say that you have 1,500 hours' worth of work on your work queue, and your team is getting through 100 hours' worth of work each week. That means that unless something changes (which it will!), you will complete the last item currently on your queue in 15 weeks.

Of course, you expect that other things will be added to the queue in the meantime, and that some things might be removed, but your best estimate today is that the thing at the bottom of the list will be completed 15 weeks from now.

As you learn more about your team and your product, your estimates should get better, and the speed with which you get through work may improve. With a simple burndown chart like this, you can always give your best estimate of when a specific piece of work will be completed based on the speed with which your team gets through work (velocity) and how far down the work queue that item is. (Henrik Kniberg explains this beautifully in the 'Product Ownership in a Nutshell' video. If you haven't watched that yet, now might be a good time.)

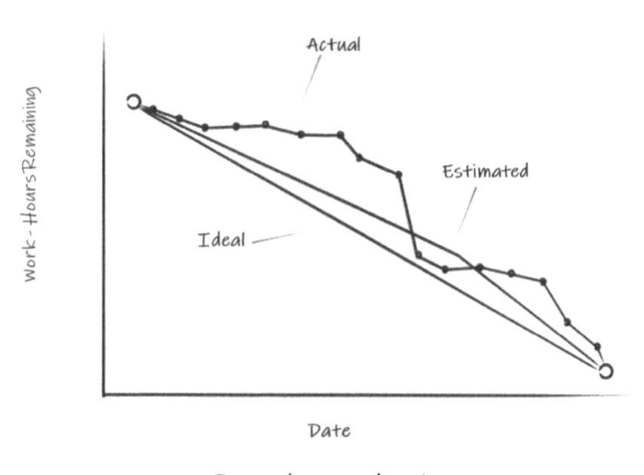

Burndown charts

Gantt Charts

Gantt charts are how project managers tell people when things are going to happen in more traditional waterfall projects. They are the first thing that pops into many people's minds when they think of a project plan, and they are quite a dangerous tool if used incorrectly. The problem with a Gantt Chart is that it sets people's expectations about future events as if they are set in stone. When a stakeholder sees a Gantt chart that says, 'we plan to go live on 18 March', they start to assume that this is a fact they can rely on. In some industries, and for some projects, this is OK. Housebuilders tend to hit their timelines often. Projects that have been run before or where the timelines are the most critical thing, like Christmas planning in a retailer, tend to stick to their timelines and one of the other variables (usually scope, cost, or quality) is compromised to make the timelines possible.

However, for complex projects, where you will be making decisions along the way about what to include, how to solve problems, and which risks to spend resources on, the Gantt chart is something that needs to be communicated very carefully.

I would recommend – very strongly – that for these types of projects, you make it very clear, from the start, that the plan is not a guarantee of delivery. It will change, and the timelines you are presenting now are simply your best estimate of what is going to happen. The level of uncertainty in your plan should be reflected in the risks and contingency you have captured for your project. As the project continues, and risks either reduce or increase, the level of time contingency shown on the plan should reflect that.

I would strongly recommend that you set people's expectations that the plan is going to change from day 1. You are going to update the plan every week, and some things will move more quickly than expected while others will move more slowly than expected. A great way to do this is to make it clear that you don't have the whole plan on day 1 of the project.

Presenting the Plan Too Early

One of the most tempting things for a project manager is to present a plan that covers the whole project far too early in the process. I've seen projects set up to fail from day 1 because the plan that was presented at the start set unachievable expectations. Project managers are often backed into a corner to provide a 'go-live' date early – either because somebody important needs to tell their boss when something is going to be complete by, or because a timeline was committed to as part of a sales process.

If time is really the only important thing on a project, you can probably hit the timelines. Unfortunately, it turns out that there are other important things, like making sure the product works, keeping the costs of the project down, or not having the whole team leave because you put unreasonable demands on them. The project manager needs to be careful about how they present their plan for the project, and the contingency and caveats that they include in it.

Presenting the plan too early

I would strongly recommend making sure that your plan has the right amount of contingency in it from the start. That contingency should be tied to the risks. As the risks are mitigated or resolved, the contingency shown on the plan moves up and down, and the future dates move as well. We'll talk more about contingency later on, but showing it on the plan is a good thing.

Train your stakeholders to expect plans to change, and they won't be surprised when the go-live date has to shift to the right because of a decision you are asking them to make. If you don't train your stakeholders to expect this, you should anticipate being put under a lot of pressure later in the project when difficult decisions need to be made. Remember: Risk management is your friend. It provides a reason for changes in the project's schedule, costs, and scope. If you are not transparently and actively managing risks, expect a bumpy and unpleasant ride!

The Plan for a Plan

OK, great, so you should be careful about presenting a plan too early, but your stakeholders want to see something! They want to know that progress is being made, and they want to know when they will have an idea of delivery dates. An old consulting trick that I picked up through being in this situation on many projects is the 'plan for a plan'. If you explain to stakeholders that you need to do some work on figuring out the approach, scope, team, and all the other aspects of the project, they are generally happy enough to allow you some leeway at the start of the project. By simply stating what is going to be happening over the next few weeks to allow you to come back with a longer-term plan, you can often take the sting out of the conversation on 'why don't you have a plan yet'.

The plan for a plan

Set up the workshops you need, give time for the discussions with the team, allow for hiring or onboarding the right people, and present a plan for getting to the main plan. Once people know that they will see a more extensive plan on a specific date in the future, and when they can see what you are doing to get there, they tend to be much more supportive.

Timeline Contingency

If you are managing and communicating your risks well, timeline contingency is a great way of helping to show your stakeholders the possible impact of those risks coming to pass. Each risk on your RAID log should have a description of the impact if not sufficiently mitigated. By putting these impacts on your Gantt chart, you help to make the potential impacts much clearer for stakeholders. They can see that by not prioritising the help you are asking for, they will force the project to go live later than they want.

Timeline contingency is controversial. People don't like to be forced into facing up to the reality of a project's risks, but it is imperative if you want to make sure that the project hits its timelines. You can offer your steering committee to remove the contingency that you have included if they take some sort of action – spending more money, putting more resources onto the team, reducing the scope etc. Contingency is there to drive the conversation about what the project needs, and to make sure that everyone is under no illusions that there are real impacts if those needs aren't met.

Include Dependencies

Much like risks, dependencies are a key element to call out on your timeline. As your plan develops over time, your dependencies can become risks that need contingency. If you are waiting for another project to complete before you can do something on your project, and that other project is running late, that should be reflected in your plan. Your stakeholders should be aware of the potential impact, and maybe they can throw some more resources behind that other project if necessary.

Cadence – Checkpoints & Project Meetings

A great thing to show on the plan is the key project meetings and checkpoints. Project meetings like steering committees or funding approvals are key focal points of many plans. Getting them on the same plan as the project's work will show everyone what to expect and help to make sure that they happen and are taken seriously.

If you are running an agile project using Scrum, put the sprints on to the plan. If you are running a waterfall project, put in the 'phase complete' checkpoints. People like to see progress. Things completed give confidence that the project is on track and moving in the right direction.

Another great tool for the PM is the 'go/no-go' decision point. You can put these through the plan at key points – for example, the end of the design phase or the anticipated first release of a minimum viable product. Go/no-go decision points give your stakeholders confidence that they will have the final say on the project's big decisions, but they also make it clear that they need to be engaged as they will be on the hook for deciding to push back a release if things don't go well.

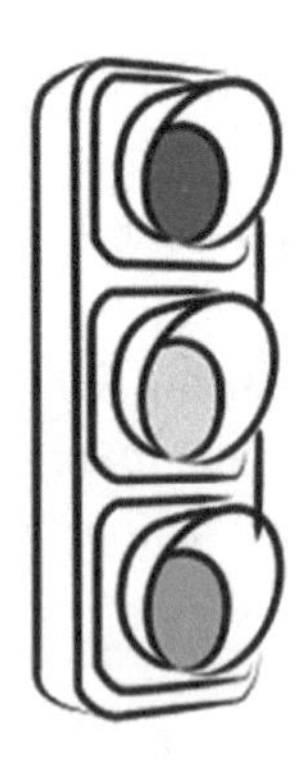

Go/No-Go decision points

Moving and Cancelling Meetings

Another mistake that many project managers make is moving or cancelling key meetings. This happens because either an important stakeholder is unable to attend or because some crisis has hit the project and the plan or update to the stakeholders is unclear. Cancelling or moving meetings under these circumstances, especially on short notice, is a big mistake. If a meeting can be moved or cancelled once, it can be moved or cancelled again. I've seen meetings chased through diaries for weeks and eventually cancelled because they became the time in people's diaries that could be moved to give way to more urgent things. If you have decided to set up a meeting, you need to make sure that it is attended and successful; otherwise you lose some of your credibility as a project manager.

You'll notice I said '*if* you have decided to set up a meeting'. That's because people often set up too many meetings. In my experience, fewer, better-facilitated, and better-attended meetings are a much better option than more meetings that are poorly attended and move around the diary. I included a lot of ideas earlier in the book on facilitating meetings because, if you can make the meetings you have work for you, your impact as a project manager is magnified many times over.

Work vs Duration

The work in the plan is not the same as the duration of the activity. You need to be clear in your head about which one you are talking about in any situation. Work is the amount of time that a person will take to complete the task if they are doing nothing else. Duration is the length of time from the start of the task to the end of the task.

If I'm driving from Paris to Dakar, the work of the trip is the actual driving. I need to drive 12,427 km, and if I average a speed of 60 km/hour while I'm driving, the work is 207.1 hours or 8.63 days. However, that's not actually what's going to happen. I can't get into the car in Paris, drive for 8.63 days and get out again in Dakar. Other things need to happen. I'll need to stop to eat, sleep, stretch, and look at the scenery. Let's say I manage to drive for an average of six hours per day. The duration of the trip is going to be 34.5 days – a very different number from the amount of work.

It's the same with your project. Your plan needs to reflect not only the amount of work that will be done on each task but also how that work will play out over time. As a rule, I'm yet to find anyone who can do productive 'head-down' work in a busy company or project for more than about six hours a day. Most people (including myself) only manage about three or four. This is because of toilet breaks, team meetings, phone calls, questions from colleagues, questions to colleagues, somebody turning up with doughnuts, and the delivery driver dropping off a package. Therefore, if your team estimates that a task will take eight hours, and you put that down on the Gantt chart as one day, you are setting everyone up for failure.

I prefer to estimate the work as work (total hours spent on the task while focused) and the duration as duration (multiply the work by the team members' average productivity and the number of team members working on a task). For single-person tasks, the work is always less than the duration. If you can split a task across multiple people, sometimes you can make the duration less than the work. Imagine 100 people counting ballot papers on election day. They get through 200 hours of work in a couple of elapsed hours.

If you are explicit about your assumptions on this calculation and open about how you came up with them, both your team and stakeholders will be able to get behind your estimates, and they will turn out to be much more realistic.

Chapter 8
Quality – Not Messing Stuff Up

Projects need the right level of scrutiny

The quality of the product that you are building is another lens that should frequently be on the project manager's mind. As with all the other lenses, this is an art rather than a science. I've never seen a project go live without some level of risk acceptance or live defects, and unless you work in a highly sensitive industry like medical devices or aeroplane software development, you will have to decide what level of quality you are working towards. In those industries, defects can be fatal to human life and there is (rightly) very little appetite for accepting defects in the final product. However, in most situations, you are trying to find the balance between quality, cost, and time that best suits the projects' needs. As my dad explained to me when I was making my first DIY projects, 'You can have it good, you can have it quick, you can have it cheap. Pick two.'

The iron triangle

https://doi.org/10.1515/9783111271149-008

He was, as with most of the advice he has given me over the years, absolutely right, and his way of explaining it has helped me over and over again to make good decisions about trade-offs between these three things. Not only does it help to make good choices, but it also helps massively in terms of presenting options to stakeholders.

In most situations where a decision is required, one of these three characteristics will need to give way to the other two. If you need something to be quick and cheap, quality is going to suffer. If you need it to be good and cheap, it's probably going to take a long time, and if you need something to be quick and good, then you had better get your wallet out!

As an impactful project manager, this balancing act is a good way for you to frame the project's decisions and come up with options for people to choose from. Whatever the problem you are facing, it can usually be solved by spending more time or money or by accepting a lower-quality outcome. Which options you choose will then depend on the project's circumstances and your stakeholder's priorities.

Too often, project managers don't see this trade-off and they have a one-dimensional view of decision-making. Some people end up repeatedly pushing the timelines. Others are always going back to their stakeholders, asking for more money and resources. Project managers rarely consider a reduction in quality (or scope) when that is often the easiest lever to pull. I can't tell you which one to choose, but next time you have a significant challenge on your project, see if you can come up with options that use each of these characteristics differently, and you are more likely to come up with an option that your stakeholders will be OK with.

What is Quality?

Quality relates to how well the project's output relates to what the users want and need. In traditional projects, quality was tested by how well the product met the requirements that had been laid out at the beginning. This is often done through testing or 'quality assurance' towards the end of the project. If the product or service meets the specifications, then it is of high quality. While this makes sense in a manufacturing context where you want all the products to be the same, it is less applicable in the world of bespoke projects, where almost by definition, you are doing something for the first and only time. Quality is a much more ethereal concept for complex projects. Traditional measures like the number of outstanding defects, or the number of requirements met by the project are OK for giving stakeholders the illusion of control, but impactful project managers tend to think in terms of the project's outcomes rather than its outputs.

If you look at the companies that have been successful in the past 20 years, many of them are able to change direction and react to new developments extremely quickly. Netflix started out by posting DVDs before changing tack to become the world's largest streaming service. Amazon noticed that they could sell data centre services better than anyone else and built a huge business out of it. Facebook built its business to an enormous scale before figuring out how to monetise it.

The same is true of many projects. The outcomes of the project are uncertain, and not changing direction when a great opportunity or a dangerous risk presents itself is just a sign of corporate inertia or individual stubbornness that does not add value to the business. That's why I'm such an advocate of a stakeholder approach to quality. The project manager should stay really close to their stakeholders throughout the project, keep them informed of what is going on, and seek their feedback wherever possible. Tools like customer satisfaction surveys and focus groups are extremely powerful, both for figuring out whether you did a good job and working out what the next piece of work should be.

I've also noticed through my many years of experience that projects almost never finish completely. There is always something else to be done that wasn't thought about or scoped in the project's early stages and that only came to light towards the end. Businesses are constantly changing and moving forwards (at least the good ones are) and the project landscape is constantly changing as well.

This is a little tricky for project managers and those who train them because it's such a difficult concept to nail down. Proving that you have fixed all the high-priority defects feels really good. But having zero defects is irrelevant if no one is using the product because it's not available through the right channels.

Of course, a system that has bugs in it is frustrating and will produce bad outcomes, so it's important to test it in the traditional ways, but great project managers also look for more opportunities to make the product better all the way through the project.

The Cost of Quality

One of my first projects as a developer was in online grocery retail. I was part of a team that was responsible for a major update of a website and fulfilment system's pricing functionality. The project was complex as we had to build dozens of different pricing mechanisms – buy one get one free, X% off, £1 off, three for the price of two etc. It was also made more complicated by the fact that some things were sold by unit (one apple) and others were sold by weight (500 g of broccoli). We went through the normal waterfall process of building out an enormous requirements traceability matrix, going through the design phase for each of the requirements, then building everything and eventually putting the whole release live one night.

We had spent a few months in change request purgatory (see chapter 4), and we spent a lot of time coming up with scenarios to test the different calculations that needed to be done. The timeline of the project extended out, and eventually we were in that awkward phase where you have to go live, but you know there are still issues. We did the best we could to document the issues we were aware of and tell all the stakeholders about them. We got the sign-off to go ahead and, over a long weekend, we put the system live.

Everything seemed to go fine to begin with, there were a few minor bugs, which we resolved quickly, and there was a great night out with the project team to celebrate a successful and very difficult release.

A couple of days later, the mood shifted. We started to hear reports of weird things happening in the supply chain to the stores which fulfilled the online orders. One store received several tonnes of bananas that they weren't expecting, another store received a huge quantity of broccoli, and a third store received the whole Southeast region's supply of butternut squash. At first, we were confident that it was nothing to do with us. We'd been looking at pricing and weights and measures on the website, which was a tiny proportion of the goods that were going to each store. However, we diligently started looking through our code to see if there was anything that could have caused it.

While we were doing this, there were crisis meetings with the supply chain department, the stores, and the warehouses, and a lot of very senior people started getting involved. My boss at the time, Matt, was involved in some of these meetings, and I learned a lot about management from the way he handled this crisis. He was obviously under huge pressure to find out what had gone wrong, but he kept that pressure on himself. None of it fed down to us, and he did everything in his power to support his team while we looked for the issue.

After a couple of days of searching through the code, one of the other developers found an override programme that had been put into the system when it was first built by a diligent developer who was future-proofing the site for the growth of online shopping. That developer had put in an override for the supply chain. If the amount of an item ordered online was greater than the whole weekly order for the store through the tills, the volume of the item bought online would be automatically ordered from the warehouse and sent to the store. That developer was envisioning a steady growth in online ordering that may, at some point in the future, start to overtake in-store shopping.

What we'd done (it turned out that this bug was completely our fault) was miss a decimal point in our vegetable weighting calculations for this obscure piece of code. Instead of ordering 1000 g of butternut squash – enough for a nice Sunday lunch for a big family – our bug had put through an order for 1000 **kg** of butternut squash – enough to feed a small town. When multiplied by 1000, even the small amount of food that was ordered online was triggering this override frequently and causing chaos across the supply chain of a major supermarket!

Within a few minutes of finding the bug, we were able to put in a hotfix which resolved the issue, but the damage was already done. Hundreds of thousands of pounds worth of fruit and vegetables had been sent – in huge quantities – to certain stores, while lots of other stores received none at all. One store manager was giving bananas away for free, while all the other stores in his region had no bananas to sell!

The cost of the bug dwarfed the cost of the project that we'd been doing, and there were some very red faces all around!

Fortunately, the relationships that our senior team had in place and the overall size of the companies meant that the whole thing was little more than a blip in a profitable year for both organisations, but this kind of bug could have destroyed a smaller company. We learned a valuable lesson about testing that week, and we have a great story to tell about it.

A few weeks later, the managing partner of the consulting group that I was working for at the time was at a major retail awards ceremony with around a thousand people at a sit-down meal. By this stage, the story of the supply chain issue was well known in the industry and had been reported in several newspapers. He was sitting next to the CEO of the supermarket chain, chatting away. The dinner was being served, and everyone else received a lovely plate of prawn cocktail to start with. Our managing partner didn't get a starter, though, and the supermarket's CEO started making a big fuss about the fact. After a few minutes, when the whole room had been made aware that our MD didn't have a starter, there was a great fanfare from the speakers in the hall. In the ensuing silence, two waiters entered the room carrying a gigantic silver bowl over to the head table. As everyone strained to see what was going on, the CEO of the supermarket stood up and announced that our MD's starter had arrived – the world's largest-ever bowl of butternut squash soup!

An enormous bowl of butternut squash soup

Product vs Project Management

The realisation that product development is never complete, particularly for software and services, has led to a growing movement of 'product management' rather than 'project management'. The shift in mindset is quite dramatic. Instead of working towards a defined end point, as you do with a project, product managers focus on two very different timelines – now and infinity. They focus on making the highest-value, lowest-effort changes that will benefit the users of their product as soon as possible, and they focus on the strategic opportunities that will make it possible for their product to get better forever.

Lots of companies still run projects, and the project itself is a very useful construct to help focus attention and resources on a particular area for a period of time, but I think that if a few more project managers learnt a bit from the world of product management, they would find their outcomes (and careers!) improved dramatically.

Technological Advancement

I have managed projects that changed legacy systems that were 30 years old, and I've led projects that used brand-new technology. The difference in the experience is immeasurable. Something that might take months from people with deep expertise to change and test on an old mainframe could be done in seconds, with very little risk, by someone with limited technical understanding of a modern low-code technology stack. Fifteen years ago, I spent weeks writing HTML and JavaScript code just to get a website up and running for a new business venture. Last week, I spent five hours with an expert in the Wix website platform. Not only did I have the website up and running quickly, but I had set up training courses linked to video conferences, discount codes, a subscribe to our mailing list function, and a credit card payment facility. And it all works!

There has always been a difficult decision for software projects around whether to buy a vendor-built product or build your own from scratch. Nowadays, there is an extremely powerful third option, which is to buy a platform like Salesforce or Microsoft Dynamics and hire expertise to develop what you need within that platform.

The world of work has also changed dramatically. I found the expert in wix com on the Upwork platform, and he was happy to sit with me on a video call from his home in Cyprus for five hours over the course of a week, answering all my questions and getting me up and running with the platform. All for a cost of $125. Years ago, I would have had to hire a full-time team locally to develop the functionality I needed, costing hundreds if not thousands of times more and taking a lot longer.

The pace of technological change is so fast that the waste created from out-of-date technology decisions is one of, if not the costliest hidden issue with a lot of projects. Seriously, check out a YouTube video on how to use wix.com. You'll be blown away by how much you can do with no prior experience.

DevOps

In the last few years, this technological advancement has spawned the DevOps movement. Put simply, DevOps is about automating as much as you can of your process. You can now automate testing, code reviews, releases, and load balancing of servers – pretty much all the things that used to take projects a lot of time. And if you are using freelance tools like Upwork and Fiverr, you can find expertise to help you at the drop of a hat.

Finding Experts

It was a Friday lunchtime, and our IT security and infrastructure expert was away on a two-week holiday. We'd just run a virus checker on the servers of a small company that we'd recently bought, and the news was not good. There was a serious issue with malware on the server, and it needed to be dealt with immediately.

My initial fear was that we would have to call Keith on his holiday. This was too big an issue to let sit for the weekend. It was possible that there was a data breach, and we knew there was a vulnerability. No one else on the team knew what to do. Fortunately, I knew how to find an expert in short time.

I simply took a copy of the error message that we were receiving from the software and set up an advert on the Upwork platform, offering to pay someone $100 to join myself and our infrastructure manager on a call and explain what the problem was and how to solve it.

Within 20 minutes, we had five proposals, which we looked through and picked a chap, Derek, with the perfect CV for dealing with this problem. We set up a video conference, and within one hour of finding the problem, we had a world-class expert telling us how to solve it. The fix turned out to be straightforward (It's easy when you know how!), and we had it done within three hours. Our expert wrote us up a short paper on the issue, the fix, and what we needed to do to avoid it in the future, and we were finished for the weekend by 5 p.m.!

If we hadn't been able to find Derek, we would have either had to call one of our hardest working colleagues away from his relaxation time – something that I avoid doing at all costs – or spend the weekend ourselves googling around and reaching out to people in our network to try to figure out the solution.

The difference in the success of people who find and use expertise well and those who don't will be exponential over the next few years. If you want to not just double but multiply your team's effectiveness by 10×, I would seriously suggest you get yourself an account with a worldwide freelancer site and look for opportunities to help your team out by employing deep expertise for very short periods of time. Life is exponentially easier when you are sitting on a video call with someone who has seen the problem before.

Finding expertise for micro projects

Making Progress – The Three Ps

There are three powerful concepts that can help you show progress through your project with real, tangible outputs that your stakeholders can see. If used effectively, these can give a real sense of momentum to a project as well as de-risk the overall deliverables and ensure that quality issues do not have a large impact. This is a great way to bring a bit of the agile iterative delivery into an otherwise waterfall project. Let me introduce you to the three Ps: prototype, proof of concept, and pilot.

Prototypes

Wherever I can, I advocate the use of experiments in project management. Doing some work to find out more about a situation is very often a great use of resources. You can find new ways of thinking about a problem, discover new approaches and solutions, and move a situation forwards. The great thing about experiments is that you are not putting a lot on the line. You are deliberately doing something small and potentially 'throw-away' so that you have more information to make bigger decisions or allocate resources more effectively.

Prototyping is a great way of doing experiments to find out more about the product you are building. Whether it's a web page drawn on a flip chart in a workshop, or an app built using one of the many prototyping tools available online, you can very quickly put something in front of stakeholders that gives them a flavour of what you are working towards. People are visual animals, and a prototype brings the product to life in a way that a big list of requirements simply cannot do. People use a different part of their brains to review a prototype, and you will get valuable feedback very early in the project that can help to steer you in a much better direction.

Proof of Concept

A proof of concept is a great brand to put on your early release to the public. Somewhere between a prototype and a pilot, it can help you answer some of those big outstanding questions that your team are wrestling with. People tend to be quite forgiving with bugs and issues in a proof of concept, and you will find out a lot about your product and your client nice and early in the process.

The Power of the Pilot

- When it comes to quality, one of the best experiments you can do is the pilot release. Sometimes called a "beta" release. This is about exposing the project's outcome to a small, often supportive community of end users to find out if there are any glaring issues or omissions. Pilots have several big advantages:
  - You can set the expectations of the pilot group that they are getting an early view of the new product so that you can get their feedback. They are likely to be much more forgiving of any issues that they encounter, and, in many cases, they will be flattered and even more engaged with your company because you have asked for their input.
  - You can show progress to stakeholders who are putting you under pressure. People like to see something 'live'. With a pilot, you can make the point that the functionality is live, even if there are still significant issues that need resolving.
  - Once you are in the pilot phase, you are constantly learning. It will be much more valuable to get feedback from people who are using the product for what it is intended, as opposed to people who are trying to think of all the angles before they can really see the product in action. You will get lots of ideas for easy improvements that could make a big difference to the final product.

The Three Ps and the Project Manager

When it comes to how to use the three Ps, you need to think about your stakeholders as well as the product itself. Using prototypes, proofs of concept, and pilots can demonstrate progress while minimising the risk of reputational damage by releasing something that isn't ready yet. You might choose to use one, two, or all three of the Ps in your project depending on the context or, if you are running fully agile, your iterations from minimal viable product onwards will do much the same thing. The power of the three Ps is the opportunity they give you as a project manager to brand parts of your overall schedule and show tangible progress when it might otherwise be difficult. Use them wisely!

All of these techniques will help you to find problems before they have a chance to create too much damage. That is what driving quality is all about – balancing the effort that you put into making it right against the risk of it being wrong.

Chapter 9
Team – Your Most Valuable Resource

A great team plays to the individuals' strengths but also aims to get better every day

Most of what we have talked about so far is coming from the angle of what you should do as a project manager. It's all important, but it is all for nought if you are not able to leverage the most powerful resource that you have at your disposal – your project team.

Teams can be small or large, stable or transient, seasoned or inexperienced, and how you manage them will make an enormous difference to your project's success.

As the project manager, there is a good chance that you are one of the more experienced members of your team. It's your job to make sure that everyone else uses their time well, stays aligned to the project's goals, and is not getting overwhelmed by work. As you know from the Foreword to this book, I have personal experience of becoming overwhelmed by too much work, and it was a terrible experience that I would like to help you and your team avoid. If a few more project managers take more responsibility for making sure that their teams are operating in a sustainable way, with sensible working hours, holidays, and time with their loved ones, I will be delighted with this book's outcomes.

But creating a sustainable balance for your team is not easy.

Like everyone else, when the COVID-19 pandemic hit in March 2020, I found myself having to manage my team through virtual communication only. While we were well established in our methods by that time, this seismic shift in the way we were forced to work nearly caused a couple of breakdowns on my team. Even

https://doi.org/10.1515/9783111271149-009

after the lessons from my own experience, I nearly missed the fact that two of my team members were operating outside the structures we had put in place and had started to take on far too much work.

The first indication was when one of the guys started turning off his camera on our calls. I had advocated that everyone should keep their cameras on whenever possible because I value the human connection of being able to see people, and them being able to see me. When Rob (name changed) started to keep his camera off on a couple of meetings, I didn't think too much of it at first. Some people were working in their kitchens with laundry hanging up behind them; others were working from beds and sofas and just didn't want everyone to see into their personal lives. We were all reacting to the new ways of work and finding our way.

After a couple of weeks, though, I started to notice that Rob was not completing work that had been agreed with him. A few people started complaining to me that he had promised things and then had not followed through on them. He had always been hard-working, so I started to get concerned. I set up a 1:1 with him to find out what was going on. He wasn't a direct report of mine at the time, so this was quite a big step coming from the chief information officer, but the situation was unusual, and I needed more information.

When he joined the video call, he once again left his camera off. As it was just the two of us on the call, I insisted that he turn on the camera, just for that meeting, and when he did, I was quite shocked with what I saw. He was unshaven, had bags under his eyes, and looked overwrought and haggard.

As we talked, I found out what had been going on. Since we had closed the office, everyone had moved over to Microsoft Teams as the main communication tool. Rob was one of the guys on the team who could do a lot on the main company system and everyone in the company knew it. As they figured out that they could now 'chat' directly with Rob through Microsoft Teams, a lot of people had stopped asking for their work through the sprint planning process and were going directly to Rob with their needs. He was quite a junior member of the team and was not good at saying no to people, so his list of work grew exponentially. I had no visibility of this because other people were still requesting work in the normal way, and Rob had not told either his manager or me what was going on.

Alongside the overwhelming level of work that was now coming his way, Rob was dealing with the stress of the pandemic, not being able to see family and friends, being locked in a small flat by himself every day, and not really having any support around him as his family was from a different part of the country.

The moment I figured out what was going on, I was able to take proper action. I immediately told Rob to take the rest of the week off and put a note on his 'out of office' message that if anybody needed anything urgent, they should come directly to me. Yes, that's right. If you wanted a simple change like a new field on an online application form, you now needed sign-off from the CIO! Guess what happened .... Only two people came to me! Everyone else had been putting pressure on Rob to get things done that were neither urgent nor particularly important. Things could wait a week or two, and they could be managed through the normal processes.

The two that did come to me were quickly dealt with by challenging the complexity of what was being asked for, and by coming up with much simpler 'stop gap' solutions that did enough to keep the clients happy until a proper piece of work could be scheduled and completed.

Rob ended up taking the next week off as well, and by the time he came back, we had farmed out a lot of his work to several other people, including a team in India that we had been building up to take on more work. Anyone who complained about the work was sent in my direction so that I could explain to them the pressures on the team and how their piece of work fit into the company's overall needs. Their work would be prioritised against everything else we were doing and would be done at the appropriate time. Rob came back and kept his camera on, and we were able to get the processes we'd had in place before lockdown working again using the new virtual tools that we had been getting used to.

Shortly after this, I noticed that another member of the team had started leaving his camera off on calls. I met with him and he was suffering from the same scenario. I took the same approach – take time off and escalate to me if anyone had a problem with using our standard process. Within a few weeks, we had trained the whole of the rest of the company to go back to using the prioritisation meetings and the rest of the Scrum processes we had in place, and the team members were able to proceed on a much more sustainable footing.

I would never have forgiven myself if any of my team members had ended up in the situation that I had gotten myself into a few years previously. Even under the extraordinary circumstances of a global pandemic, it is our responsibility as managers, colleagues, and human beings to keep an eye out for others and make sure that whatever else is going on, they are OK.

Productivity

Have you ever had the experience of getting into a flow state? "Flow" is that elusive feeling where you are so focused on a task that everything else falls away into the background. You are thinking through the problem, working out the angles, and making progress. Whether it's in writing a steering pack, solving a coding problem, or working through your risk log, once your mind is focused on that task and you are in the 'zone', you can create lots of value in a very short time. It's enjoyable, productive, and rare!

In the modern world, what often happens in these situations is that an interruption takes your attention away from that key task. It's a colleague coming up to your desk to ask you a question, that email or text message that makes you think about a different topic, or simply running out of time because that 11 a.m. meeting that you have to go to is coming up. This apparently trivial problem is one of the most pervasive and damaging productivity sappers, and many people on your projects will have to deal with it every day. The difference in output between someone who gets four uninterrupted hours to focus every day, and someone who is (or could be) interrupted at any point is enormous. Notice, I only said four hours. It's unrealistic to expect most people on projects to get much more time than that for focused work. Even though many of us work eight hours a day (often more), there are team meetings, questions from colleagues, coffees, toilet breaks, brainstorming sessions, helping the new guy, filling in your timesheet and so many other interruptions.

As the project manager, it is your job, your responsibility, to make sure that the people on your team can use their time effectively. A lot of this comes down to how you manage and coach them. The rest of it comes down to how you set up the environment, the communications, and the access to your team. Unless you are thinking carefully about this problem and actively managing it, you will find that the tasks you allocate to people simply do not get done, or that your team have to work long hours to meet the timelines that you agree to.

There are a few simple tips that can really help you to make the environment more conducive to effective work:

Environment

How you set up the project's physical environment is critical to how people use their time. A lot of offices nowadays have an open plan feel to them. People have collaboration spaces and there is a buzz of activity and noise. But unless you are the CEO, there is often nowhere quiet to get your head down and focus on a complex task. Since the announcement of the COVID-19 pandemic in 2020, most office workers have figured out (had to!) how to work from home. In many cases, the dial has shifted from too much interaction and distraction to not enough.

There has been a lot of debate about the 'right amount' of time in the office vs time at home, and many companies are still figuring out the balance. I have a secret for you. Whatever your company decides is the right balance of working at home vs working in the office, if they set a strict policy, it will be wrong for most people most of the time.

As the project manager, you have great power to negotiate on behalf of your team members to make sure that they not only get the right balance for themselves, but that you get the right balance for the project – and guess what. It can change every week! Depending on the stage of the project, you might need the whole team in the office for an intense back-to-back 10 days of detailed workshops and team building. Or you may have team members who have everything they need to simply get their heads down and write process maps for days on end. Balance this with people's need to limit the amount of commuting they do, pick up the kids from school, and play for their local netball team on a Tuesday evening, and the problem becomes very complicated.

While the overall problem of figuring out where everybody should be at a given time is complex, there is a simple way to solve it. Trust people to manage their own time and locations! I like to talk to my teams about the four different work environments I mentioned previously (commons, cave, collaboration, and contemplation), and what kind of work to do in each of them. Once they understand these concepts, the conversation becomes much more sensible in a weekly 1:1 about what work they will focus on for the week, and where they plan to spend their time.

Time-Boxing

Parkinson's law states that work expands to fill the time available. This is something that I certainly have found to be true. Very few people have the discipline to finish an assignment well before a deadline, and those that do often spend hours and hours tweaking and rewriting things, adding very marginal value, for quite a lot of effort right up until the deadline to hand it in.

That's why time-boxing is such a powerful tool. By allocating a specific amount of time to a task and making sure that it is complete and demonstrated by the end of that time, you can ensure that your team are consistently working towards a known deadline. If you emphasise the behaviours that you want – action over procrastination, urgency over lethargy, and progress over perfection – you will be surprised by how much work can be achieved in a short amount of time.

At the end of the short period that is allocated to a task, you can do a review and make sure there isn't anything blocking progress and that the task is heading in the right direction.

Time-boxing is great at a team level, say in Scrum, where a two-week sprint is often the length of a time-box. But it can also be extremely valuable at a much more granular level. I have often set time boxes of five or even three minutes in a brainstorming session for people to get their ideas down on paper. Very often, the most valuable time is that first few minutes of focused effort.

However you are using time-boxing, it's really important to remember that by fixing the amount of time given to a task, you are flexing one of the other dimensions of task management. Either quality or scope will have to flex to hit the deadline. Time-boxing forces you to make continuous decisions about the scope of what you are doing and the level of quality that you go to. Sometimes, you'll do a lot of things quite quickly ('good enough is good enough') and sometimes, you'll do fewer things very well ('no mistakes'), but by making active decisions on which approach is appropriate, you are much more likely to use your resources effectively.

Fit in the Big Things First

Have you ever complained that you are just too busy to do something important but not urgent? It's one of the most common problems that many people face, and it comes from a failure of prioritisation. In Western cultures, being busy is widely seen as a badge of honour. There is a little bit of theatre that many of us do when we meet someone, which points to a real problem in our lives. Does this conversation look familiar to you?

Person 1: How are you doing?
Person 2: Sure, not too bad. Busy!
Person 1: Ah well, better that than bored.

The number of times I've been involved in that conversation is embarrassing. It's like being busy somehow validates us as people. It makes us feel important, ambitious, and hard-working all at once. In recent years, I've changed the way I answer that question. I start talking about how exciting the work I'm doing is, or how I'm enjoying the challenges of what I'm up to. I make a conscious effort not to use the word busy (although it does sometimes slip out). This change in mindset lets you take more control of your time and the activities that you are working on.

The number one, most frequently asked question I get from people on my training courses is how to deal with being so busy. People feel like they have way too much to do and not enough time to do it. Well, there is a very simple answer to that question: prioritise! I don't just mean pretend to prioritise by doing the most urgent thing first. I mean actually prioritise, using value, not urgency, and thinking about the long term, not the short term. Prioritisation does not only mean deciding what to do next; it means proactively and confidently deciding what **not to do at all!**

Much like we do for our teams during a prioritisation meeting in Scrum, personal prioritisation is a critical skill for all project managers (and, I would argue, all people, full stop). If you are not good at it yet, I suggest you spend five minutes on the following exercise.

1. Write down a list of all the big things that you need to do this week.
2. Estimate how much effort you would like to put against each of them.
3. Rank them by importance (you can estimate their value, or just do it by gut feel)
4. Work down the list, adding up the totals.
5. When you get to the amount of actual working time* you have this week, draw a line.
6. In your next 1:1 with your manager, show them this list and ask them if the order is correct (i.e., whether you got the order right). If they agree that the order is correct, tell them that everything below the line isn't going to happen and make sure they are OK with that. If they think the order should be different or that the estimates need changing, the two of you should have that discussion, but do not leave that conversation without agreeing on what you are **not** going to do!

** Note: remember, we are talking about real work here. Leave out time for meetings, replying to emails, talking to colleagues etc. Four to six hours of real work hours per day is about right for most people.*

This conversation, when you get used to it, works really well as a manager and as an employee. Whenever people come to me claiming to be too busy, I have this conversation with them, and we agree on what the work should be. Anything below the line becomes my problem, not theirs (at least not this week). I can walk away knowing that my team have a sustainable level of work and that they are working on the most important things for the organisation's goals. They walk away feeling supported and confident about meeting the expectations that have been set.

Prioritising the work of individuals this way makes it much clearer where the bottlenecks are in the team and what the medium-term needs are. If I am consistently having to agree that important work will not be done, then it is incumbent on me to assign more resources to that area, either by hiring someone else or by training a colleague to do that kind of work. Those things then go onto *my* 'to-do' list and are prioritised in exactly the same way.

You may have heard the example of filling up a jar with rocks, pebbles, and sand. If you fill the jar with the sand first, then try to add the pebbles next and only then add the rocks, you will have lots of air gaps in the jar. If you plan and prioritise the big rocks first then you will fit a lot more in, and, more importantly, anything that doesn't fit in will be less important!

Fit in the big things first

Distraction Audit

In today's office and home-work spaces, there are many things that can cause a distraction and reduce your team's productivity. Whether it's being interrupted by that little box that pops up when you have an email or a text message from a colleague, switching tasks is a much less efficient way of working than concentrating on one thing for an extended period. Add to that all the 'non-work' distractions that come at us from all angles – WhatsApp groups, social media, the children coming home from school, and the Amazon delivery person ringing the doorbell – and it's a wonder anyone gets any work done at all.

While you can't prevent these things from happening, there are certain things that can be done to lessen the impact, and a great way to do this is to have a discussion with your team through a 'distraction audit'. It's a very straightforward concept. Simply keep a piece of paper by your desk for a few days and note down on the paper every time you got distracted from your flow of work. Something like this:

Distraction audit

Once the team have done this for a couple of days, some themes will arise, and you can discuss how they can be avoided. Some people prefer to do this alone, and others are happy to share their distractions, but once they see how much they are getting distracted from the task at hand, they are more likely to be open to certain distraction avoidance techniques, such as:

- Turning off your email alerts and only checking emails every two hours.
- Muting all non-essential app notifications (including social networks, WhatsApp and Slack) and checking messages only when you are checking your emails.
- Agreeing periods of quiet working time, say from 10 a.m. to 12 p.m. and 3 p.m. to 4:30 p.m., when there are no meetings, and no one is allowed to distract anyone else unless it's an emergency.
- Building a list of things that you need to speak to someone about and keeping track of, then bringing them up at a regular meeting rather than piecemeal throughout the week.
- Allocating time to 'pair programming' type work where two people are solely focused on the same task, sharing a screen, and working together. This can be a great way to get through a lot of work very quickly, where there is a high level of dependency between two or three people that requires regular discussions.
- Realising that you are interrupted at 2:45 p.m. every day when the kids come home from school and scheduling that as a great time to take a coffee break, have a quick chat with them, and make sure they have everything they need for their homework.

The distraction audit is a powerful tool for helping team members figure out their own working approach, and how they can work more effectively both with colleagues and on their own.

Being Human

I am a very keen member of the scouting community. This started as a child and has been as true at the start of my career as it is now. I have gained a huge amount from scouts, and I love the idea of paying that back as much as possible. This element of my character and persona also has a pleasant upside. It gives me something to talk to lots of people about that is not directly related to the work we are doing. Most people have a positive view of scouting, and there are lots of good experiences that can be uncovered in a very short conversation. Some of my other favourite titbits to share about my personal life include the fact that I ride a motorbike, enjoy cricket, like dogs, and have three kids. Between these personal traits, I can pretty much always find some common ground with people at a human level, whatever is going on in work.

In the early days of my career, it became a bit of a standing joke on the project. At 5 p.m. on a Monday, my alarm would go off and I'd start packing up my laptop and bag. My friends on the team (they were friends as well as colleagues – we were new graduates in a consulting company, so our social lives and work lives were heavily intertwined!) would call out 'dib dib' and make scouting salutes as I left them to their work. They knew I worked just as hard as they did, and that I would be there other nights that week when they were not, and it gave us all a sense of support and community that we could help each other with our work–life balance.

As I became more and more senior, I kept this practice up, and its significance changed drastically. As a junior member of staff, I was allowed to leave early because the company wanted to show its flexibility to its employees. As a senior leader in the organisation, I came to see it as about me setting the tone and culture, and encouraging others to prioritise their own personal lives alongside what they were doing in work. As I was now a leader in the businesses I was working in, me getting up and going to scouts at 5 p.m. on a Wednesday (the evening changed when I moved to a different scout group in Ireland) gave other people the freedom to do similar things and helped to embed that culture of flexibility.

Be a human

Too many organisations pay lip service to this kind of flexibility, and too many managers do not set a positive example in this space. Why not have a think and challenge yourself to see if you can be the change you want to see in your own company's culture?

Extreme Ownership

Jocko Willink is a former US Navy SEAL who wrote the book 'Extreme Ownership'. One of the lessons in the book is that when you are under fire, it doesn't matter how you got there or whose fault it is. A leader takes responsibility for solving the problems – whatever they are. There is a powerful lesson in this for project managers. If you can think of the outcomes of the project rather than the day-to-day minutiae, your actions will be much more aligned with the project's overall success, rather than just doing what you have been asked to do by your stakeholders. There is a famous scene in the film *Superman* where an earthquake creates a fissure underneath a train track (a classic example of a risk becoming an issue!) Superman flies to the scene, bends one of the tracks back up, and uses his own body to allow the train to pass by safely.

This is what I mean by extreme ownership when it comes to project management. Whether the risk was flagged or not, whether it's your fault or someone else's that there is a problem, as a project manager, you make sure that what is needed gets done. No one else is going to take responsibility. The most successful leaders understand this, and that is why they are so successful. They get to the desired outcome, whatever the route that's required.

Extreme ownership

Give Flexibility to Get Flexibility

A project's demands fluctuate over time, and sometimes you need your team to go out of their way to help you. If you can show flexibility for the needs of your colleagues, then they will show flexibility in return.

If someone comes to you asking for an early finish on a Tuesday because they are involved in their daughter's football training but they are happy to start early on a Friday instead, I advise you to do everything you can to help them make this work. The value that they will get from being able to do what they need will be repaid in hard work and positive attitude. When you need them to spend a week in workshops in a different office three months later, they will be much more likely to help you out if on every Tuesday at 4 p.m. they got up, signed off, and had not been bothered while they were focusing on their family time. Some managers feel the need to constantly monitor their colleagues and check what they are working on. This might be necessary for very junior colleagues in low-paid work, who are not committed to the company or your goals. However, I have found that if you are doing the right things about helping that person to get better every day and to achieve what they want to in their career, they will repay the favour by working hard, and a virtuous circle of trust and respect can grow.

Give flexibility when you can – you never know when you might need it in return

There is a proverb that I like to think about in this context about storing your food in your neighbour's belly. If you were a hunter on the plains of Africa in the days before industrialisation and you came back with a buffalo, there was no way that you could eat the whole thing yourself before it went off. So, you ate some and gave a lot to your neighbours. When they had food later in the year, they would repay the favour. This concept of general reciprocity without keeping track of everything that's owed is a strong way of thinking about how you deal with the flexibility of your team's working hours.

If you can spot an opportunity to let the team leave early on a Friday afternoon in May when there isn't much going on, then they are likely to be much more open to staying late on a Tuesday night in September when there is a critical issue that needs resolving. Don't wait for them to do you a favour before you do them one. Start the reciprocity whenever you get the chance, and the culture of helping each other out will grow from there.

I am lucky to have worked in companies that allowed me that kind of flexibility. As I mentioned previously, I have always been involved in scouting, and from my very first project, I was fortunate to have the confidence to ask my boss if I could leave slightly early (5 p.m. instead of 5:30 p.m.) on a Monday night to make it back in time to lead the local scout group meetings. I worked in an extremely high-paced environment and was often required to do long hours and weekend work, but I almost always made it out on time to get to scouts on a Monday. My manager was very supportive of that.

I must have put in thousands of extra hours on projects over the years, but I always felt that it was my choice to do so and more related to my ambition for promotion and self-improvement than being put under pressure by my manager to work late. This is a subtle difference, which requires managers to recognise extra effort and thank people, but it can be a very positive dynamic for all concerned.

I say that I was lucky that the culture supported me in this, but it's not luck at all. Plenty of other people who worked for the same companies would complain about the lack of flexibility or the long hours and demands that were put on them. As an impactful project manager, I'd like to challenge you to see if you can create the kind of culture where people are supporting each other with flexibility and are comfortable to ask for help when it's needed, even if it (very rarely!) means working outside of contracted hours. The right culture can make all the difference to both personal happiness and project success when it comes to flexibility.

Traditional Leadership vs Servant Leadership

In the past, leadership was seen as something that came from your position. If you were the manager, people expected you to lead. If you were senior in the company, you had earned the 'right' to be a leader. This is still true in some organisations and was inherited from millennia of human history, when the biggest organisations tended to be military organisations. In these kinds of groups, the leader's ability was paramount. Think of Napoleon or Alexander the Great at the top of a huge organisation, setting the direction and making all the decisions.

However, as the amount of information available has increased exponentially over the last century, this kind of 'command and control' structure is being outperformed by distributed decision-making, where the general direction may be set by a figurehead, but the actual day-to-day decisions are delegated to the people nearest the information. In the 1800s, it was possible for one person to know everything there was to know about a given topic, and they could therefore put themselves in a position to make better decisions than everyone else in most situations. That is simply not possible now. Anybody can get their hands on general ideas and information very quickly nowadays, so the closeness of the individual to the actual data, the process, or the people involved becomes much more relevant than their leader's individual ability to know everything in the wider world.

As with all things, there is a balance, but for most organisations, delegating authority more than they currently do is a great way to increase their teams' effectiveness.

With the development of the Agile Manifesto, a new type of leadership has gained popularity over the last decade: servant leadership.

I find it useful to think of leadership in terms of these two competing mindsets: traditional leadership vs servant leadership.

Traditional Leadership	Servant Leadership
Sees leadership as a rank	Sees leadership as an opportunity to serve others
Uses power and control to drive performance	Shares power and control to drive engagement
Measures success through output	Measures success through growth, development, and outcomes
Speaks more than listens	Listens more than speaks
Believes it is about them	Understands it is about the team

Good leadership is all about your team

Servant leaders see themselves as responsible for helping everyone else to be great at their jobs. They remove obstacles, encourage, coach and motivate their colleagues, and are focused on ensuring that the whole team performs in a sustainable way. It is an empowering mindset, and it makes working a lot more fun, so it's well worth thinking about how you can make your own leadership style a bit more servant-like.

Traditional leadership

Servant leadership

Motivation – Autonomy, Mastery, and Purpose

Back in 1943, Abraham Maslow created his hierarchy of needs, building up from physiological and safety needs, through a sense of belonging and self-esteem to self-actualisation and achieving one's full potential. This is a pretty good model and has been used for over 70 years by HR professionals to try and figure out how to motivate people.

In most projects nowadays, the bottom of the pyramid is well covered, and project managers can focus their energy and attention on the top of the pyramid. Particularly, project managers should pay attention to the areas of friendship, feelings of accomplishment, and achieving one's creative potential.

While a good understanding of psychology and motivation is valuable to a project manager, the practicalities of motivating your team were summarised beautifully by Daniel Pink in his 2010 book 'Drive'. As a way of thinking about your colleagues and motivating them, this is one of the best models I have come across.

Pink argues that by enabling just three behaviours, most people's work can become much more fulfilling and enjoyable. I tend to agree with him. Certainly, the lack of any of the following three factors can be a hugely demotivating condition for people.

Autonomy

Autonomy means the ability to make decisions that impact your day-to-day work. This means that you have a level of control and influence over what you are doing. If you are part of the team that decides what you work on and can argue your case as to what should be done next, you are more likely to enjoy your work than someone who is simply given task after task without having any say on their to-do list.

Autonomy

Mastery

Getting better at what you are doing is highly motivating. If you can see your skills improving and your knowledge growing, you can imagine a better future for yourself. This factor ties in with the growth mindset that all successful people have, whereby they never want to stop learning. Once you have mastered one skill, there is always another one to work on, and if people are not getting this growth in their jobs, they are likely to start looking for it elsewhere.
(While we are talking about mastery – if you know anybody who would benefit from the ideas in this book, maybe you could send them a recommendation, or, even better – buy them a copy.)

Mastery

Purpose

Purpose is perhaps the hardest of these three motivation factors to get right. It can take real leadership to explain the 'why' of a project, but it is crucial. If your team doesn't know why they are doing what they are doing, motivating them will most likely be a struggle. Before sharing the purpose of your work, the place to start is to understand it yourself. I have known people who have been at odds with the ethics of the company they work for. They took the job because it paid well, but they had reservations about what that company was doing, or why it was doing it. These people can lose motivation very quickly even at senior levels, and once they start thinking about the ethics of their work, they soon have one foot out of the door.

I don't have an answer to creating purpose where there is none. Pretending that a company's purpose is to help people get out of debt when they are really trying to lend those people money at exorbitant interest rates, or to save the planet when they are increasing investment in fossil fuels is, in my opinion, disingenuous and sucks the life out of work. My advice if you work for one of those types of companies is to leave and try to find something that aligns more closely with your own ethics.

Purpose

If, however, you do work for a company or department that aligns with your own beliefs, purpose becomes a huge driver. One of my own driving goals is to help people get better at what they do. I spend a lot of my spare time as a scout leader and I love teaching my own children, so when it comes to picking what I do at work, an element of training and teaching is essential to me finding purpose in a role. Other people are motivated by the company's output, such as building great houses for people to live in if you work for a construction company, or creating drugs that will save lives in pharmaceuticals. Whatever the purpose of your company or division, as an impactful PM, it is your responsibility to figure it out and make sure that it aligns with what your team are doing, or to use your influence to change it.

Many organisations have a vision, mission, and values statement. Try to track down yours and see what it says. It should give you a good idea of your company's 'why' and ethics, as well as how you can communicate them to your team. If your organisation doesn't have one, it is a worthwhile exercise to spend time with your team and stakeholders on creating the vision, mission, and values for your project. That way, you don't only give your team a 'why' but give your team members an input on it as well to make their purpose truly their own.

Drive

The great advantage of Dan Pink's model of motivation is that it is memorable and actionable. If you can keep those three words – autonomy, mastery, purpose – in your mind in every interaction with your team, you will start to spot opportunities to improve their motivation all over the place.

Delegating decisions, asking people for their opinions, and giving them control over how they go about their work are great ways to dial up the autonomy in people's jobs. Mastery is also easy to help with as a PM if you take it seriously as a goal. Can you introduce someone to a mentor or a mentee? How about sending them on a training course, or simply telling them to use a couple of hours a week during work time to learn something about their work? Purpose is the one that is difficult to create out of thin air, but if your company or your project has a great purpose that aligns with your own ethics, spending time talking about it, elevating that purpose, and making it more visible are powerful leadership qualities that will help motivate your team and yourself. Doing this will be positive for your career as well!

Team Make-Up

How you build your team is critically important to success in your project. The traditional model of a co-located team working five days a week in an office is great in some circumstances, but there are situations where you can improve the team's productivity by adding certain resources at certain points in the project. Much like the description earlier in the book about finding expertise, building and shrinking a team to fit the project's needs is much easier than it used to be.

While most projects will still have a core team working full-time on the project, impactful project managers know how to ramp up expertise and capacity at the right points in the project's lifecycle.

For example, a few years ago, we needed to roll out a system to 600 people. The tasks to get set up on the system were simple once you knew how to do them, but we were struggling to convince people to stop their busy day jobs and perform the four steps that were required. The task was complicated by the fact that the users needed to enter their passwords at one point in the journey, so we could not simply do the set-up for them.

The solution was relatively easy in the end. Instead of using expensive project team members to sit with each user and get them set up on the system, we hired a temp for a couple of weeks. We taught him how to do the task, gave him a list of people to contact, made sure he had a direct line to the expert if he needed it, and let him go with the work. He was able to reach out individually to every user, spend three to five minutes with each one to get them set up, teach them the basics of the system, and move on to the next person.

Instead of trying to align diaries and train everyone formally, which would have been extremely difficult, this ultra-flexible approach of just fitting in whenever people had a few spare minutes worked beautifully, and we completed the task in just a couple of weeks. Plus, all the users were delighted because they had a genuinely positive experience and did not get frustrated with the new system before they'd even started using it.

Deploying low-cost resources in this way can be great, but it also works with very expensive resources. I needed someone to talk me through the process of proofreading, editing, and publishing this book. Within a few hours on the Upwork website, I had found a couple of very experienced editors who were happy to talk to me for an hour and help me figure out what to do. It was easy money for them, and great for me to get access to their expertise in micro-chunks. Meeting and getting input from someone with that level of expertise would have been very hard any other way. If you really want to have an impact on your project, then – as well as getting the most out of the team you have in front of you – you should also consider what value you can get from the rest of the interconnected world!

Use the interconnected world

In the 20th century, single great thinkers have been replaced by research communities and teams. Enrico Fermi was once described as the last person who knew everything. As an impactful project manager, whenever you need expertise that isn't available, you should be thinking creatively about how you can get that expertise at the right level and for the right amount of time. Whether it's a short-term contract, a training course, research on the internet, or simply buying the book, knowledge really is power and how you use it makes a big difference to your success.

Give People Great Tools

As I am writing this book, there is enormous buzz about Large Language Models (LLM) and Artificial Intelligence. I have seen the hype cycle of this kind of technology before, and very often, the overall impact is much less than the hype. This time, however, I believe it is different. The LLM AIs are so easy to use, and so practical, and they have so many obvious use cases that they are clearly going to change a lot of the work that we do over the coming months and years. The technology is moving so fast that almost anything I write about it will be out of date by the time you read it, so I'll stick to making a more general point.

Whatever the technology that your team are using, as a project manager, it is your responsibility to make sure that it is fit for purpose. At the very least, it should be a help rather than a hindrance, but I try to set the bar much higher than that.

Your team should have the tools they need to do a great job. Whether it's a powerful DevOps toolkit, process mapping software, extras screens, or a comfortable chair, investments in the tools of the working environment are well worth making. They will help your team become more productive, avoid de-motivation, and create much better outcomes for your project.

Celebrating Success

While we're talking about success, it is crucial to celebrate success when it happens. In my early career, whenever we finished a big project, there was a big party. We went to a posh restaurant, followed by a nightclub to really let our hair down. On one occasion, after a particularly difficult project, we were given a weekend ski trip. These celebrations drew a line under the project or phase of work and made everyone feel appreciated. Your company's culture may not be so flamboyant, and budgets may not be as extravagant as we had back in the early 2000s, but there is no excuse for not having a celebration when your team has completed something important or difficult.

A few beers and soft drinks in the office with crisps, pizza, and a bit of music can be just as good as an expensive restaurant. The key is that people feel valued and appreciated for the effort that they have put in. Impactful project managers celebrate success!

Saying Thank You!

Saying thank you is even easier than organising a party, but it is sadly underused by so many project managers. An email to someone, noticing the good work they have done, and CC'ing their manager and a few senior people can mean the world to that person. I know it does when it happens to me! If you really want to make this impactful, adding one or two lines about what they did and why it was important will make the gesture even more powerful. If you want to go even further, a handwritten note, possibly with a small gift, can be memorable and will be appreciated even more than an email.

Some of the most impressive project managers I have met build gratitude into their weeks. I know one leader who has a 30-minute section in his diary every Friday when he stands back from whatever is going on and says thank you in different ways to different people. His team and colleagues love him for it, and everyone speaks very highly of him. That is such a simple, impactful way to spend your time.

For the last few years, I have taken the opportunity at Christmas to send a handwritten Christmas card to every member of my team. The cards did not just say 'Happy Christmas'. They called out in a few sentences some of the big things that I appreciated about that person's work during the year. Sure, it takes me a couple of days to go through the activity, but it is time well spent. It makes me reflect on what my team members have achieved in that year, brings home just how far we have gone together, and lets them know they are appreciated at a time of year when that really counts.

Chapter 10
Stakeholders – Who They Are and How to Make Sure They Are on Your Side

Stakeholders are people too!

You can't avoid it – the biggest part of being a project manager is working with people. Impactful project managers learn how to deal with people. They are constantly thinking about their team and their stakeholders, how to communicate with them, what their point of view is, and whether they agree or disagree with a decision. This is the most overlooked and under-taught area of project management. It does not matter how good your Gantt chart is, or how well you manage the project's individual tasks. If you are not working well with your greatest resource, your project will fail, and your reputation will suffer.

With this in mind, it is a good idea to think about who your stakeholders are. A stakeholder is anyone who has an interest in the outcomes of your project. They can be the senior manager who commissioned the project, or the user of the end product. Anyone who has influence over or is impacted by your project is a stakeholder. Some people will care deeply about how the project goes, and others will have just a passing interest, but the lens of the stakeholder is one that is well worth looking through regularly.

People Are People!

When I was an undergraduate learning about economics, we were taught about things like supply and demand, and game theory. These ways of thinking about the world simplify the human being down to a 'rational actor' – someone who makes good decisions based on perfect information and is always right. While some people

https://doi.org/10.1515/9783111271149-010

like to think of themselves in this way (myself included), they are completely and utterly wrong! The problem with treating people as if they are perfectly rational is that they are not! In business, people's relationship with rationality is very sketchy indeed – especially when you overlay the fact that your view of rationality is just as wrong as theirs is!

When you stand back and think about it, this becomes obvious. Colleagues are forever showing themselves to be imperfect. They don't reply to emails, only attend certain meetings, talk about issues behind our backs rather than confronting them directly, underestimate work, overestimate capability, forget things, stick to their guns in the face of overwhelming evidence etc., etc., etc.

When people are starting out as project managers, one of the biggest mistakes they make is to treat people like machines. Only with years of experience, and often after expensive coaching, do PMs eventually start to manage people rather than tasks. Hopefully you are already a people manager, but there are a few tips that I believe can be helpful. All of them involve dealing with people by moderating your own behaviour rather than trying to change theirs which I wish someone had taught me when I was starting out as a project manager.

No Arseholes

There are no arseholes in business.

Nobody.

Whatever you or other colleagues might think about them, not one single person in your organisation considers themselves to be an arsehole.

So I don't consider anyone to be an arsehole either, and taking this position is extremely beneficial. Instead of seeing people as arseholes, I prefer to think about the ways that they are different from me. What do they know that I don't? What do I know that they don't? What pressures are they under? What priorities do they have? What resources do they need? As soon as I change my way of looking at people who initially might seem like arseholes, I can start to see ways of interacting with them much more constructively.

Everybody is different for sure, but if you come across a lot of arseholes in your day-to-day work, then I would strongly recommend that you take a look in the mirror to see what is causing the issue. When two people meet and walk away from the interaction with the view that the other person is an arsehole, what has happened is a failure of communication. You have both failed to see the world from each other's point of view. If you still think someone is an arsehole, you have more work to do to make sure that you see their point of view, or that they see yours. The former is easier!

The Only Behaviour You Can Control is Your Own

I do have some dictatorial powers over my children. If I say they can't have a sweet, they can't have a sweet. If I say, 'go to your room', they do. But this is the only area of life where this is true, and I find that when I use these powers, things tend to go badly. I have long ago learnt that telling someone to do something in work is not a great way to get things done. The best way to get someone to do something is to get them to want to do it.

As an individual, you can decide what to do. You can decide to write an email or pick up the phone; you can decide to make the controversial point in a meeting or hold it back for a private conversation. These are the soft skills of stakeholder management, and they are well worth refining and working on. What you can't do, though, is make someone else behave differently. If you challenge someone's knowledge in front of a room full of people, expect a defensive reaction. If you back someone into a corner and make them do something they don't want to do, expect there to be negative consequences when they are speaking about you with colleagues at the water cooler. Instead of barging through as a command-and-control-type project manager, the impactful PM will have a lot more tact and nuance and will moderate their own behaviour to achieve the outcomes they want.

Listening is the Most Powerful Stakeholder Tool

It's an old adage that you have two ears and one mouth, so you should listen twice as much as you speak. One of the most powerful weapons in your armoury as an impactful PM is your ability to listen. Listen often, listen well and listen with an open mind. If you want to really understand someone's position, you not only need to listen to them, but you need to understand them. To do this, the tools of active listening are your friends. Listen to the point they are making, then play it back to them in your own words. Ask questions, clarify things, and understand the background to their points. If you do this well, they will not only have been listened to, but they will *feel* listened to and, more importantly, you may well start to change your own mind and position on the subject.

Project management is not about knowing all the answers on the first day. Impactful project managers are constantly learning about the situation, and they have the confidence to change their opinions on things when they discover new information.

Different Ways to Engage Stakeholders

A few years ago, I was running a major project for a foreign exchange (FX) trading team. I had several key stakeholders who were paying for the project and cared strongly about the outcomes. Near the beginning of the project, I sat down with each of the stakeholders and started to build up a picture of what they wanted from the project. At the same time, I was mentally taking notes on how best to engage with each of them, and it turned out they were all different. One of the reasons that the project went so well was that I realised how important each of these stakeholders was, and I changed my behaviour to match each of their needs.

Graham

Graham was a dedicated and hard-working trader on the FX desk. He was an absolute expert in the area and had strong opinions about the details of the FX trading application that we were building. He knew his customers really well and knew what they wanted. He also had time dedicated to the project and goals from his leadership team to not only complete the project but also make the new business that would be using it a success.

All this made him the jewel in our stakeholder crown. He was influential, energetic, and knowledgeable. I negotiated hard with the office manager to situate a couple of members of my team next to him and gave him full access to everything we were doing. He was invited to meetings about the details, he was included in emails about key questions, and each team member spoke to him multiple times each day.

Joe

Graham's boss and the owner of the budget, Joe, was supportive of the project but nervous about how the new system would impact his team and his existing business. He wanted to be kept up to date so that he was never surprised by anything but was very busy with other projects and priorities.

For this reason, Joe loved my status report. Unlike many of my project management peers, I was diligent about producing a status report every week. The status report went to a list of about 15 different stakeholders, and I knew that most of them didn't read it. Despite that, I still produced the status report by 4 p.m. every Friday, and even when I was on holiday, I made sure my team still updated it and sent it out right on time. Joe read the status report over his coffee on a Saturday morning before his game of golf, and I always made sure I was in the office early on a Monday morning before things got busy. If there was anything in the status report that Joe was interested in or worried about, he would come and find me at my desk at around 8:30 a.m. and we'd have a chat about it. Joe joined the monthly steering meetings, and whenever there was anything controversial, I dropped him an email and we went for a coffee to discuss it.

Karl

Karl was the head of the department and the project's sponsor. As such, he operated at a political level in the bank. He was constantly negotiating with his peers and was also involved in a significant restructuring programme. He was extremely busy, and my project could have been better timed, in his opinion, if it had been left until the following year. Karl trusted Joe and Graham but was wary of me as an external consultant.

He also received the status report, but I don't know if he read it in detail. I had a monthly 30-minute catch-up with him and Joe to appraise him of the project and ask for any support we needed. He met with Joe on a daily basis, and so when there were key messages that I needed Karl to hear, I would draft a short summary of the issue in a written email to Joe and ask him to bring it up. On a couple of occasions, Karl was interested enough to ask for a follow-up meeting with me, but for the most part, he was happy that Joe was in control and kept him informed.

Jane

Jane was extremely busy as the head of IT security for the bank. She was responsible for a portfolio of over 50 projects and cared strongly about making sure they all did all the right things in terms of IT security.

Her team had produced a 94-step checklist that needed to be completed before a project could go live. Instead of waiting until the end of the build phase, I took that spreadsheet and started tracking it as part of the overall project status. Each week, I would report how many of the steps were complete in the status report. Jane was very difficult to get hold of, but one of her team was able to work with my team on the checklist, and we remained green on her radar throughout – even when we had significant other issues on the project – because she knew we were taking her priorities seriously.

Peter

Peter was the solution architect with overall sign-off of the project in terms of the technology. He was assigned to my team for half a day per week at the start of the project, which was not nearly enough to get everything we needed done. While his knowledge was extensive, getting him to complete any of the deliverables was a real challenge because of his time constraints.

Because of these constraints, one of the earliest risks I raised to the steering committee was the lack of availability of a solution architect. Within a few weeks, I had upgraded it to the most significant issue on the project as it was seriously impacting our ability to make decisions and drive our work forwards. With the support of the steering committee, I was able to negotiate Peter's time on the project up to one day per week, but we also hired an external designer, Darren, who did not know the bank well, but knew the technology well enough. I tasked Darren to make the absolute most out of Peter's time. Whenever we had a meeting with Peter, Darren was there. He'd prepped the questions that we needed to get answered, he'd researched the options and he'd reviewed the systems. Peter was able to come to the meeting and be highly effective because most of the work he was responsible for was done for him.

The FX Traders

The system was going to change these people's work, and they were concerned that it would take some of their power away by removing the personal connection with their customers.

Graham was the key to this group. He was friends with the team, and they trusted and respected his opinion. He made sure that he went for coffees and drinks with the team and sought their input and feedback on the design. At certain points in the project, we demonstrated the prototypes and got their input into new functionality that was required. Towards the end of the project, we had a comprehensive training plan, and the roll-out of the system took their concerns and feedback on board by making sure that we went slowly and onboarded the customers, a few at a time.

The Customers

The small- and medium-sized businesses who would use the system were the reason why we were doing the project in the first place. They wanted FX trading to be simpler, quicker, and cheaper.

We held multiple focus groups, demos, and pilots with the customers and when we rolled the new system out, we got the traders to go and meet them face-to-face to explain how to use it. This re-enforced the bond between the traders and the customers and gave them an opportunity to feed into the system and change the design.

There were many other stakeholders on this project, and for each person or group of people, I sat down and figured out how best to communicate with them. While the project had its challenges and ended up taking longer than originally planned, all the stakeholders were supportive throughout. And because the right people were able to get behind the key decisions, my team and I were seen as a highly capable project team that had delivered really well for the bank.

Engage different stakeholders in different ways

Everyone's Point of View Counts

No one has the whole picture. For any complex project, it is simply impossible for one person to have all the different pieces of information and be able to make all the decisions. The technical person will have a view on the technology, the salespeople should know about the customers, and the leadership should have a view on the context and the organisation. Gathering all these inputs into your overall approach and plan is key to the project's success. While it might be easier not to engage certain stakeholders, or to simply allow them not to be involved because they are 'too busy', doing so leaves you open to the risk that something that you can't deal with will come up later in the project. Managing your stakeholders in a way that makes it easy for them to give you what you need and stay involved in the project is fundamental to the project's overall success, and something that impactful project managers keep at the forefront of their minds every day.

You need a range of views to make a successful project

Using People's Time Well

One of the easiest ways to annoy people, especially busy people, is to use their time poorly. Here are some common examples that you will see repeatedly. The impactful project manager avoids all of them as far as possible.

- Cancelling meetings – especially at the last minute
- Meetings that are too long
- Allowing meetings to get side-tracked
- Emailing when it should be a phone call
- Calling when it should be an email
- CC'ing too many people on an email
- Not CC'ing the right people on an email
- Replying to all when a reply to one person is more appropriate
- Interrupting people
- Starting meetings late
- Finishing meetings late
- Not responding to messages
- Lack of preparation for the meeting
- Not completing what you said you would do
- Not providing enough information
- Providing too much information

As you can see from the list, it's a tricky balance to make sure that you are doing the right amount of a certain activity. It takes experience and thought to make sure that you include the right people on an email chain. It is hard to decide whether to pick up the phone, send an email, or wait for the next meeting to discuss a point. This is a nuanced world, but the key is to stop for 20 seconds before a communication point and think through the best way to engage with the next action.

I have seen email chains that went on for weeks without any progress when all that was required was a simple 10-minute meeting with the right people in it. I've seen entire meetings wasted because the right information was not available in the room. Your job is to pick the right tool for the job and do it with elegance. Here are a few tips that you might consider.

Save Up Your Discussion Points

If you need to speak to someone about a lot of things, just allocate a section of your notebook to keep track of those things. When you come to your next 1:1 with that person, not only have you not annoyed them with multiple questions throughout the week, but you look proactive and organised by having an agenda for the 1:1. Very few people do this, but I'm always impressed by those that do.

Shorten Meetings

Why set a meeting for an hour when 15 minutes will do? Why keep talking when you can finish the meeting and give everyone time back in their diaries? If you use agendas, time-boxing, and facilitation techniques well, you can significantly reduce the amount of time required in a meeting and make sure that it is more productive to boot. A quick summary at the end of the meeting, or even a short email follow-up with the decisions and actions made, can take less than five minutes but can be the difference between a productive meeting and a complete waste of everyone's time.

Review Your to and CC Lists

Quickly checking the recipients of an email before you hit send or 'reply all' is a great way to make sure you don't annoy people by either including the wrong people or missing someone out. Here are a few tips on email etiquette:

- If you are changing the context and subject of an email – change the title and start a different chain.
- Consider a 'branch email' if there is a smaller group that needs to discuss one specific point, then set off a different discussion with only that group.
- If you want a senior person to know that you have something under control, and keep them out of the detail, you can BCC them on the email chain and use wording like **'BCC'ing Mary (CEO of the company) so that she is not included in the detailed discussion. We will present the outcomes and decisi-**

ons required at the next steering meeting.' This is a great way of explicitly valuing a senior person's time and a great way to boost your own reputation as a 'Do-er'. Just make sure you don't drop this ball!

- If you need a response, include a call to action for a specific person and give a deadline.

Setting Up Meetings

- Use the scheduling assistant. I am astonished at how few people check other people's diaries when setting up meetings. The scheduling assistant in Microsoft Outlook is crucial to getting people to attend your meetings. If you don't know how to use it, go and learn right now.
- If you can't see people's diaries, make it easy. Sometimes putting a little table in the email for people to reply with their thoughts works well. The reply all's will build and the people who haven't responded will get a little nudge each time someone else responds. For example, if you are looking to figure out a good time for a meeting with a few people and you don't have access to their diaries, something like this can help:

Name	Tuesday, 9–10 a.m.	Tuesday, 3–4 p.m.	Wednesday, 9–10 a.m.
James	Available	Available	X
Jane			
Mark			
Dave			
Ava			

Give a practical solution to the little problems that get in the way

- Set a brief agenda. Putting three bullet points on a page about what will be discussed in a meeting takes only a few seconds. It gives everyone confidence that the meeting will be effective and helps people to be prepared for it.
- If a senior person is too busy to attend, ask them to send a delegate instead. This is a great way of finding the actual person who can help you with your project, and not getting stuck with someone who is too far away from the detail. It has the added benefit that if someone's boss has asked them to take on a task, it tends to have more weight than if they are asked by a peer or a project manager who needs something from them to be involved in a project that they don't care strongly about.

- Make it clear why this meeting is valuable to them. Giving a meeting a title like 'Go/No-Go Decision Meeting' or 'Stakeholder Input Meeting' has many benefits. If people don't attend, they can't accuse you later of not including them, and most people don't want to miss out.

Getting Sign-Off

Sometimes as a project manager, you need a formal sign-off from a stakeholder. This can be extremely difficult to get as many people don't like putting their name on something where there is risk. It can also be difficult to get people to pay enough attention for you to be confident that they are signing off on something. Here are a few tips to help.

- Only include sign-offs **if they are necessary.** If it is likely that the scope of the project will change over time, then agile methods can soften the 'pressure' on Sign-off. These allow you to change direction in the future, so the permanent nature of sign-off decisions is much less intimidating for stakeholders.
- Make clear what the implications of sign-off are. If you are closing out design, be clear on how changes to requirements will be managed after this sign-off.
- **Set a deadline.** 'If we haven't heard back by Tuesday, 12 October, sign-off will be assumed.'
- **Allow them to delegate.** 'If you would prefer a member of your team to sign off as they are closer to the details, please let me know who to contact and make the introduction.'
- Make it easy. Some companies need specific wording to meet regulatory requirements. If that is the case, add the wording to the email so that they can copy and paste it. If you make them type it out or go and look it up, it's another reason that makes the sign-off feel like more work than it is. You want to avoid that feeling if possible.
- Sign-off's often don't have to be performed over email. Sometimes having a show of hands in a governance meeting and minuting the sign-off decision can take a lot of the effort out of chasing individuals. You need to make it clear beforehand that the meeting will include the sign-off, and that the minutes are very clear, including who attended, but otherwise this can be a great way of getting people to focus their attention for just long enough to get the sign-off you need.

Talking of sign-off – I'd love to get your opinion on this book so far. If you have enjoyed it, I would be eternally grateful if you would take 30 seconds to leave a review wherever you bought it so that others can find and benefit from it as well.

Decisions

When my wife and I got married, we agreed that I would be in charge of everything. All the things. I'm in charge of them all.

(Apart from decisions.)

She does the decisions.

All of them!

Decisions

I use this to get a laugh at my talks, but also to make a serious point. As a project manager, it isn't really your job to make decisions. You need to make sure that decisions get made. You need to make sure that the right people get behind the decision, and you may well be providing recommendations and ideas on what the decisions should be. But you shouldn't make them.

Senior people need to feel that they have control over projects. If they have made the decision, they are much more likely to throw their weight and resources behind it and help it to turn out successfully.

The other thing to realise is that decisions are on a scale from easy to hard. Easy decisions are either low impact or obvious. The decision on what to have for lunch is easy because it is low impact. If you have the soup today and don't like it, then that's OK; just have a sandwich tomorrow. You can even leave the soup and order a sandwich instead. It'll cost you a bit more money, but you can easily rectify the situation.

The other decisions that are easy are the obvious ones. You don't step out onto the road when a car is coming because it's obvious that the car will hit you, with bad consequences.

When it comes to decisions, you can make them easier by either reducing the impact of the decision, or by making it more obvious what the right answer is. You can also spend some effort improving one or other option to help the decision become more straightforward.

Agile approaches reduce the impact of decisions by allowing you to make lots of little decisions and change course if you find out you need to. They also emphasise the importance of experimenting and finding out more information. If a decision is too difficult or controversial, spending some time to find out more information is often very valuable.

I once joined a company where one of the most important things I needed to do was to make a decision over a certain piece of software. The options were:

- **Option A** – Continue to build the system with a development team where the relationship was fractious, the costs were high, and progress had slowed, but where the underlying product was great.
- **Option B** – Throw away what we'd done and start again with a new vendor who was promising us lots of great functionality.

The problem I faced was that I was new in the door, and everyone else had been wrestling with this decision for months. They had gotten completely stuck, with two firmly entrenched camps polarised around each option. Rather than just picking one and annoying half of the stakeholders, I took the approach of finding out more information and improving the options as much as I could.

We allocated a small but tangible budget (about 5% of the overall budget of the project) to an experiment, a hackathon where we would directly compare the two options. Team A would see how much progress they could make on Option A in two weeks, and Team B would do the same with Option B. In the meantime, I also went out of my way to understand the issues with the development team in Option A and to learn a bit more about the company in Option B.

After two weeks, the two teams presented what they'd done, and I shared my observations.

- **Option A** had made significant progress. They had changed the ways of working to a much more iterative and engaged method, they had gone for drinks together with the vendor and improved the relationship, and I'd paid the vendor the money they were owed for previous work, which had been held back because my predecessor hadn't been happy with progress.

- **Option B** had made very little progress. We'd also discovered that the company was new to our market, very small, and reliant on one developer, who had been away on holiday for part of the hackathon.

All of a sudden, after just two weeks and spending only 5% of the project budget, the decision became much, much clearer. Option A was a good option, if we worked with and repaired the relationship damage with the previous vendor. Everyone could see this, and the board was happy to sign off on the investment required to pursue this approach. This went on to be a hugely successful project, with the company winning an enormous contract off the back of the technology we'd developed and the system winning awards for the way it changed healthcare recruitment in Ireland.

The best thing about this approach was that, while we had spent 2.5% of our budget on throw-away work with Option B, everyone was now 100% behind Option A and dedicated themselves to making it a success.

When it comes to decisions, another thing to remember is that once you have made a big one (and I always prefer making them as small as possible), you can't go back and find out whether the option you didn't choose would have been better. This means that the harder or more important a decision is, the more effort you need to spend on getting everyone into a place where they support the decision.

Many project managers make the mistake of having a strong opinion on what the right option is far too early in the process. They then try to persuade others that their way is the right way, rather than listening, finding out more, and going on a journey with everyone to figure out the best answer. That's why I like to recommend that you treat your stakeholders like I treat my wife and let them make all the decisions.

Note: I'm lucky. My wife is great at decisions, and we agree most of the time. When we do disagree, I take it as my husbandly duty to understand why she is taking a position. Nine times out of ten, she persuades me. The other times, I'm able to give her some more information that she wasn't aware of and change her mind, or I simply realise that the decision is not anywhere near as important as the relationship and go with her plan. We are happy and there aren't any arguments, which is amazing!

Difficult Conversations

Sometimes there is just no alternative. Something has to give, and people are avoiding making a decision or facing up to the reality of what is going on or needed. In these scenarios, it is time to steel yourself for a "difficult conversation".

The first thing to remember with a difficult conversation is that it is much better to have it than to ignore the problem. Whether it is a behaviour in a colleague that is causing a problem with the team, or a tough reality that a key stakeholder isn't facing up to, as the project manager, it is your job to make sure that the situation is resolved. No one starts out their career relishing these discussions, and many people never develop the skill of addressing them. Issues that could have been dealt with through empathetic coaching or transparent prioritisation can sometimes continue for months or even years and can undermine many of the good things that the team are achieving.

Difficult conversations, like anything, get easier with practice, so my advice is to just start having them. The first couple may be daunting, but with a few simple tips, they are much more likely to go well, and there is something extremely satisfying and freeing about dealing with an issue through an up-front conversation rather than letting it fester and cause problems down the line.

So how do you go about having a difficult conversation? The first thing to do is to spend a little bit of time preparing for it. Just a few minutes can be enough, but you need to be clear in your head what the point of the conversation is. If someone keeps promising the world and failing to deliver. Your goal is to help them either stop promising or start delivering. If someone has unrealistic expectations of a colleague, your goal is to help them understand the reality of the situation. If someone is coming across as snappy and aggressive, your goal is to help them find ways of working more effectively with people.

Once you have it clear in your mind what the problem is as you perceive it, the next thing to do is NOT TO SOLVE IT!!!

If you are at all like me, your first instinct will be to give the other person the solution to their problem. Tell them to be nicer, or more realistic, or that they need to work harder or promise less. While this might feel like the obvious approach, it has been proven time and time again that it is a terrible way to change other people's behaviour. How do you like it when someone else tells you how to act? Not great, eh?

So how do you have the difficult conversation and address the problem without jumping in and solving it? The answer is simple – Listen!

There is not a single person in the world, no one at all, who sees themselves as a bad person, and there are very few who find it easy to recognise their flaws. It is also extremely important to bear in mind that your view of the problem is only one view. Other people may perceive no problem at all, or that the problem lies with someone else, or (surprisingly often!) your own behaviour! Even if you can agree on the existence of a problem, the cause may be something completely different from what you were thinking. That angry person may be going through some personal difficulties at home, the lazy person may simply not know how to do part of their job, and the stakeholder who refuses to face up to reality may have a completely different agenda that you are not aware of that is served by their behaviour in relation to your project.

Difficult conversations are therefore much more about finding out information than giving solutions. If you can ask a few questions, sensitively and with empathy to find out why things are the way they are, then you will start off the conversation on a much more positive footing. Your job is to get the person to open up and bring you around to their way of thinking. You need to see things from their perspective before you can have a hope of resolving the issues.

Once you take this approach, the problem-solving part of the discussion either becomes much easier or may not need to happen at all. If you can understand their point of view, then you may be able to make some simple changes in your own behaviour or the approach the project is taking that will accommodate or learn from their concerns or issues. Just by having the conversation and listening to their point of view, they are much more likely to feel that they have influence and power over resolving the issue, and they will very often make a few small changes in their own attitude or approach without needing to be told what to do.

Just having the conversation well, with empathy and genuine listening, will often be enough to resolve most issues and there are a few simple tips to help make sure that it goes well.

- Pick your time – Low stress, not in the heat of the battle
- Pick your location – A nice coffee shop near the office rather than in the middle of the open-plan work area might be a good idea
- Pick your audience – Do not try and have a difficult conversation in front of other people. This is a 1:1 kind of a deal; adding an audience into the mix is almost guaranteed to make it worse
- Pick your timeline – Some things can take a while to resolve, don't feel like you have to get it all done in one conversation, starting is important, but so is allowing the process to progress at a natural pace
- Pick your words – Blame is bad, empathy, trust, and the benefit of the doubt are good

Difficult conversations are one of the hardest parts of being an impactful project manager, but they do get easier with practice and time, so think about any areas where you are perhaps not listening well enough and see if you can use the difficult conversation technique to make a difference. Good luck!

Chapter 11
Cost – How to Think About It, How to Discuss It, and How to Keep a Lid on It

There is never enough money

Very few projects complete on time and on budget and deliver 100% of the expected results. I make the claim when advertising my training course that impactful project managers can save between 10% and 100% of a project's costs. While this claim is deliberately controversial, I stand by it, because the role of an impactful project manager is absolutely to save their companies large amounts of waste on projects. Here's what I mean by that statement:

10% Savings

If you already have an experienced team who know your business and are highly motivated, an impactful project manager will work to make that team even more effective. As a servant leader they will trust their colleagues and spend their time removing impediments and making small course corrections that keep everyone productive. They will prioritise work, manage stakeholders, enhance communication, and reduce interruptions using the techniques in this book. Working on their projects will be fun for the project team members, who will stay with the company longer and work more effectively every day. Projects will finish earlier or have better outcomes because of the focus on prioritisation, value, and effort.

50% Savings

If your team is less experienced, or a new team that is working together for the first time, the impactful project manager will set the vision of where they are going. They will implement effective processes, coach team members, direct work effort towards high-value tasks, and ensure the project has a positive environment to thrive in. They will coach and guide team members to learn the skills that they will

https://doi.org/10.1515/9783111271149-011

need over the course of the project and then trust them to execute the tasks. They will only bring in external consultants for small, well-targeted parts of the project that are either too costly to train internal resources or can be done very quickly by an expert. When they do, they will use global networks to make sure they are hiring them in a cost-effective way.

They will limit the unnecessary documentation on the project, using processes that share information and improve decision making without requiring huge amounts of effort which do not add value to the goals of the project.

The teams that impactful project managers build will provide value to the overall organisation; they won't be afraid to challenge assumptions and will highlight risks that could have significant consequences. Stakeholders will have all the information and context they need to make great decisions using the Iron Triangle to balance trade-offs rather than wasting time and effort on low-value work just because they don't realise that it is hard to do.

100% Savings

Really James? 100% savings – How is that possible? OK, this bit of the advert is a little bit "clickbaity", but it's completely possible for an impactful project manager to save 100% of the costs of their project.

Estimates vary, but only about 50% of big projects hit their budget, only about 10% hit their budget and time, and only 0.5% hit budget and timeline and deliver the expected benefits[1]. Many projects fail catastrophically – delivering no value whatsoever. Impactful project managers can save you from these projects by identifying massive risks, issues, or dependencies early in the process. They will also make sure the only projects you start are of great value to your business because they have a very clear purpose that is well understood and discussed with the whole team and all the stakeholders.

Quite early in my career I worked on a project that should have never been started. This was in around 2005 when Web 2.0 was just getting started. The business that we were working with was called "The Canine Corporation" and was the brainchild of a very senior executive, and friend of one of the partners at the consulting firm I worked for. The team he had put together included lots of "yes men" (they were mostly men) who refused to challenge his thinking on the overall strategy of the company.

---

1 This data is from Bent Flyvbjerg and Dan Gardner, *How Big Things Get Done*. Currency (Figure 1: The Iron Law of Project Management: Over Budget, Over Time, Under Benefits, Over and Over Again).

Between them, they had come up with possibly the most ridiculous business case I have ever seen. The plan was to become bigger than WHSmith online, by just selling dog bowls, dog collars, and other dog-related paraphernalia. The vision was clear, but the assumptions were out of touch with reality, and the culture of that company was such that no one challenged the leader.

Instead of deciding to do some experiments, or even research to test the market, they jumped right in with the build of a huge infrastructure to support the potential maximum size of the business. We were putting in the same website content management system used by major corporations with thousands of products and costing huge sums in licencing and implementation costs. They wanted to configure a major accounting system – Oracle Financials – to keep track of the large sums of money they were predicting would be coming through the website, and at huge expense, they were using one of the biggest consulting firms in the world to put it all together.

I was a junior PM at the time, and I was tasked, with a team of 5 people to put in the financial system. The consulting rate for this team must have been in the order of £2,000–£3,000 per day. And we were maybe one-tenth of the overall project cost. I remember very early on in the project, I sat with the CFO of the Canine Corporation, who was also the personal accountant of the CEO, and asked him about the projections for the business. With just half an hour of questioning and probing, it became very clear to both of us that there was absolutely zero chance of the business being able to pay back the costs of the project in any reasonable timeframe. Their assumptions about how many people would buy dog bowls failed to stand up to even the most basic challenge. There was no way that this business could succeed.

After that meeting, I went to my boss to raise my concerns. He didn't take them seriously and told me that more senior people than both of us had looked at the numbers, and that my job was to deliver the financial system. I didn't take no for an answer, and on two further occasions I raised my concerns about the company's ability to pay for all the work we were doing with senior people. On the second occasion, I was taken to the side after the meeting by a senior person and told that I needed to stop causing trouble and just deliver the project.

Nowadays, I would have had the confidence to stand up to that kind of challenge, but back then, as one of the more junior members of the team, I decided not to rock the boat any further. We got our heads down, worked hard, and delivered a shiny new financial system to this company about 6 months later. We worked long hours, weekends, and late nights, and I even missed scouts a few times due to the aggressive deadlines that we were working towards. We supported each other and produced a working version of the software that could support an enormous business. We built some great friendships and learned a lot.

When it was time for the business to launch, they hired people dressed in cartoon dog character suits and kicked off a large marketing campaign, and we all watched and waited for the orders to roll in on the website. The first order came in, then the second, then the third – the system was working, but these were just test orders from various people associated with the project. Within a few hours, it became abundantly clear that no one wanted these novelty dog bowls. Days later, the website still only had a tiny number of real orders. There were crisis meetings and all kinds of negotiations, but within a few weeks, the company had gone out of business, and none of the vendors working on the project ended up getting paid for their work.

The learnings from this project have stayed with me throughout my whole life, and it was an extremely valuable experience at a personal level. However, there is absolutely no way that things should have ever got so out of control on that project. Someone at a senior level ought to have stood up much earlier and had the gumption to cancel that project and save us all a load of time and money.

If I had known the lessons from this book around transparency, prioritisation, and how to deal with people and decisions, I would have been much better equipped to have the difficult conversations early in the project, and maybe things would have turned out differently. I certainly wouldn't spend 6 months of my life now working on a project that was so fundamentally and obviously flawed, but as my dad says, "experience is worth what it cost you ", and this was valuable experience!

Cost Terminology

When I studied for my PMP qualification, I had to learn a lot of terminology that I had never come across in over 10 years on projects. A lot of this terminology is related to costs, and there was a whole section on the exam on how to calculate each of these. I'm a reasonably intelligent guy with good exam technique, an A-Level in Maths, and a degree in economics, but it still took a lot of effort to remember all these names and calculations. I'm going to list some of them here. Feel free to skip over them when you get bored.

- Earned value (EV)
- Planned Value (PV)
- Actual Cost (AC)

- Budget at Completion (BAC)
- Estimate at Completion (EAC)
- Estimate to Completion (ETC)
- Variance at Completion (VAC)
- Cost Variance (CV)
- Schedule Variance (SV)
- Cost Performance Index (CPI)
- Schedule Performance Index (SPI)
- To Complete Performance Index (TCPI)

You'll be pleased to hear that I have no intention of giving you any more detail on these cost calculations whatsoever. Not because they aren't theoretically interesting, but because in all my years on projects, I never saw them used effectively. Not once!

These kinds of cost calculations imply a level of accuracy to cost management that is only possible in extremely low-risk projects, which are quite few and far between nowadays. When I explain contingency later in this chapter, you'll see a much better way of driving good conversations about the costs of the project.

I have seen a few project managers keeping track of some of these metrics, but the only other people who understand what they mean are other people who have passed the PMP exam! No senior stakeholders or decision makers know them, and nobody on your team will understand them. If you start using this terminology you may go down a rabbit hole that sees you explaining your calculations to people with blank faces who just need some guidance on the decisions they need to make to achieve their goals for the lowest cost possible.

This is one of the main reasons why I have written this book, and why there is so much interest in Impactful Project Management Training. Learning this kind of terminology is a purely academic exercise that lends very little, if any, value to the actual business of delivering a project for your stakeholders. I had good, practical training in the consultancy that I worked for; some of the tips in this book come from that training. But the only project management training that is available to most people in most companies is riddled with these kinds of low value, high effort learning tasks that are only useful in the narrow context of passing an exam.

Don't overcomplicate the message or use jargon that your stakeholders won't understand

There are only three costs that you need to keep track of:

1. What you've spent
2. What you think you are going to spend
3. What you might have to spend if things go differently

Keeping track of what you've spent is important, and so is keeping a plan of what you think you are going to spend, but the very best conversations and decisions are needed about what you might have to spend if the risks to your project come to pass. This is contingency and without a thorough understanding of it, your project will almost certainly become one of those 99.5%[2] that fail to deliver on the timeline, cost, or expected benefits.

Contingency

One of the most contentious parts of planning a project is deciding how much contingency should be added to the effort estimate. It is also one of the most powerful and underused tools in a project managers arsenal. Used well, contingency can drive brilliant conversations about scope, risk, timelines, team, stakeholders, quality, and every other aspect of your project. Used badly, it can make you look like a lazy project manager who doesn't understand the risks to their project.

2 Bent Flyvbjerg and Dan Gardner, *How Big Things Get Done*. Currency (Figure 1: The Iron Law of Project Management: Over Budget, Over Time, Under Benefits, Over and Over Again).

There are two very bad practices that I have seen over and over again and which, for reasons I have never understood, seem to be prevalent across many different industries and projects. I'll explain these first and why they are so bad, and then we'll get on to how to manage contingency with impact.

Bad Approach 1 – Implicit Contingency

One way to include contingency is simply to over-estimate how long the work will take and hide it in the presented estimate. This is often what happens in low-trust scenarios, where the person or team doing the work is worried that they will get into trouble if they go over budget. The problem with over-estimating like this is that it hides the true estimate of the work from the real decision-makers. This means the work will be allocated inefficiently. It also reduces trust as the team's productivity appears lower than it actually is, which can lead to the unhelpful situation where people are working on things that are not valuable simply because they have to 'use up' the allocated effort.

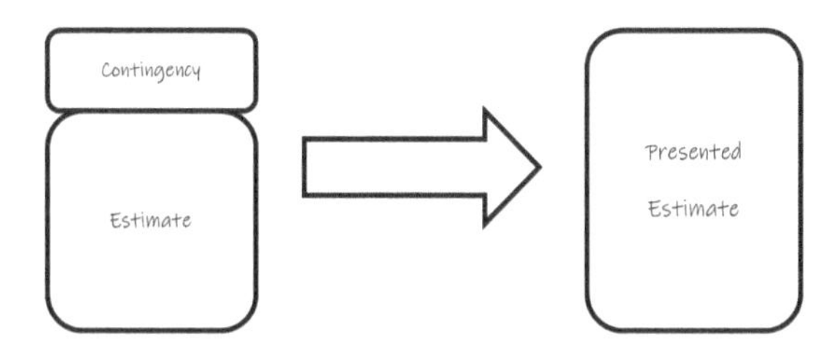

Hidden contingency

This approach is also dangerous because senior people don't get a proper understanding of how much contingency has been added. I've seen situations where contingency has been added multiple times on the same piece of work. This leads to the work looking very much more difficult and expensive than it is and driving poor decision making as a result.

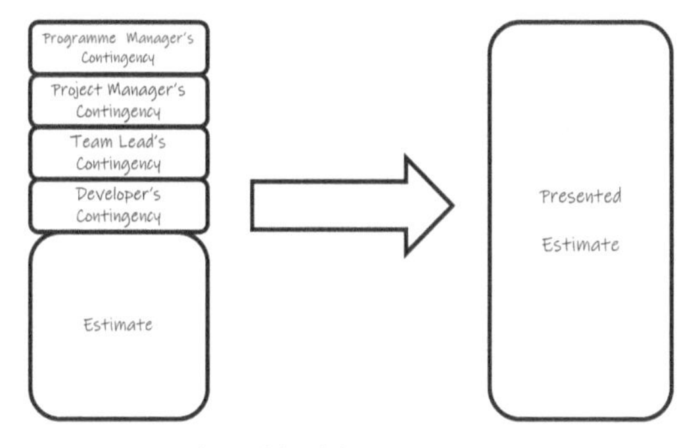

Stacks of hidden contingency

Bad Approach 2 – 'Industry Standard' Contingency

Another approach I've seen used far too many times is to simply add a percentage contingency as the 'industry standard'. This is slightly better, because at least the contingency amount is explicit and will only be used if necessary. However, it still shows a lack of problem-solving and thinking about the project's specific circumstances. Is this project more or less complex than the benchmark projects? Where did this benchmarking come from and how is it validated? What are the specific reasons for picking one level of contingency over another? When I've asked these questions of experienced project managers who use this approach, their justifications are very poor, and largely the answer boils down to "we can't be bothered to provide a rationale for the contingency, but we know we need some."

In my experience, this approach raises more unhelpful questions than it answers and is a sign of bad training of the project manager.

Good Approach – Risk-Based Contingency

The best way I've seen of figuring out what contingency to add is to relate it to risk.

Great project managers use the risks that they develop as part of their project planning to give a flavour as to what could go wrong and how much it might cost if it did. They then allocate an amount of contingency for each risk and add up all of those to provide a total contingency amount for the project.

That way, you are being explicit about what can go wrong that might require you to spend more time or money on the project. Stakeholders tend to value this approach if it's managed correctly. They can see how helping you to mitigate the project's risks will save them money and time, and they can appreciate that your risk log is not just a set of things for you to deal with – they need to help with them as well.

For example, if you are concerned that your team will not get enough access to an expert in another part of the company to be able to clarify questions they have, you can document a risk to this effect. If you then add the monetary consequences of this coming to pass (e.g., requirements will take twice as long to confirm, so we'll have to pay for the business analyst's time for two weeks instead of one) and add that as a line item on the contingency, you have suddenly given your stakeholder a really great reason to make sure that your team has access to the expert. If they don't, you'll be spending that contingency and wasting everyone's effort.

You can add contingency like this to each of the risks on your risk log, at least the big ones (remember, high impact, high probability) and suddenly you have created a risk-profile for your project in terms that everyone can understand – Money!!!

This is a great way to add 'teeth' to your risk management approach and keep the project's total costs lower than they would be if the risks you are worried about keep coming to fruition. Now your stakeholders can see what the problems are likely to be and get on with their most important job, which is helping you do deliver a successful project. It's also a great way to engage stakeholders in discussions about the project. You should be advising them to make any decisions required based on the cost of the project **including** contingency, and therefore adjusted for the identified risks of the project.

At the start of the project, you can expect to have a lot of risk and uncertainty about the overall costs. At this stage, it might be appropriate for your risk-based contingency to be 50% or even 150% of the overall project cost. But it shouldn't be calculated as a percentage. It should be calculated as an estimate and expressed as a value in money terms, just like the estimate. Your stakeholders should feel like they have some control over it and that they can reduce the contingency by helping you to manage the risks to the project.

For example, if you don't know whether you will be able to build all the functions that your stakeholders say they need using the existing systems, you can call this out as a risk and include a very hefty contingency amount in the budget for if you find out that a different system is required. Doing this will focus the minds of your stakeholders on what they really need for the project. You can talk about the things that you can and can't do on the existing system and then suggest doing some experiments to find out more about the functions that you are not clear on.

A few weeks later, you can have a really great conversation about the scope of the project, and whether to build a new system or use the existing one. If the decision is made to stick with the existing platform and de-scope some of the functions that the business doesn't really need, then you have saved everyone a lot of money and time by using risks, scope, and contingency to drive brilliant decisions about what the project does. Now that's impactful project management!

Budgets

Where the cost conversation can get much more complex and political is when you start to look at it from the perspective of the rest of your organisation. If you are following all the tips in this book on engaging your stakeholders well, ensuring that you and your team are working on the right things, getting the right people to make the right decisions etc., then you will be doing a great job of managing the project. All of that will be ruined though if you don't manage the budget and control processes of your organisation, particularly when it comes to people's expectations and promises that are made.

Most of your stakeholders are not project managers. Certainly, the finance department will have a very different view of your project. I have often heard project managers complain about procurement and finance colleagues who (in Oscar Wilde's words) "know the cost of everything and the value of nothing". It is a common problem for project managers to have to request funding from people who are not the ones who will benefit from the project, so how should you approach this challenge?

Getting Funding

Fortunately, you are already in a good place to get funding for your project. Remember back in Chapter 5, when we talked about creating a business case for your project or tasks with your stakeholders? This is one area where that activity will really show its value. As well as having a simply written and clearly articulated rationale for the work of the project to use in prioritising high-value / low-effort work, you have also had good discussions with stakeholders about why you are doing the project in the first place.

This kind of approach ought to stand you in good stead against the other projects that are being considered by the business. It should give you a place to stand in discussions about which projects go ahead and which do not. The difficult thing in these conversations it to maintain an open mind about whether your project is the best value for the business or not.

Often project managers take such ownership of their projects, that they can't see the flaws in their business cases. They believe that their project is the most important one, and that they should have lots of resources to make it a success. If you are truly looking at the overall value for the business, you need to have great conversations about whether your project should go ahead, and also what scale it should be. Sometimes, just starting with an experiment to find out more about a potential solution or market is a much easier conversation than trying to get sign-off for your whole project on day 1.

Get Stakeholders to Do the Influencing for You

If you are the only person who wants the project to go ahead, then you will have problems all the way through, and you should seriously consider how you have ended up in that situation. It probably means that either the project isn't worth doing and you have a blind spot to something that other people can see, or that you have failed to clearly explain the rationale for the project to other stakeholders.

If that is not the case, and you have support from other people, budgets, and funding are one of the most important areas to put your stakeholders to work. Most people are happy to have someone else do the legwork for them, so for the funding of your project, it may be worth seeing yourself as the facilitator rather than the driver of the project. If you spend your time building out the business case and talking it through with your stakeholders and team members, then you are building a coalition of support around the project. People's concerns can be raised and addressed, and the rationale for taking the project on can be refined and improved with the input of lots of views from around the business.

If you have good PowerPoint or document-writing skills, then so much the better, and having a good written rationale can be important, but it's the myriad conversations that you and your stakeholders will have with each other that will influence the funding decision. You should see your role as feeding supportive content to senior people to help them make the case for your project, rather than being the only advocate yourself. If you do this, then the case will be better and it will be more successful in the budgeting and planning discussions.

Stay in Budget

This is an obvious point, but a crucial one. Budgets can change, based on decisions made by senior people, but they shouldn't change without an active decision being made at the right level. If your costs turn out to be more than you anticipated, then hopefully your contingency approach has softened the blow. But even if that hasn't happened, you need to control the situation of a budget increase very carefully. Use terms like "re-baselining" the budget and make sure you have very clear, minuted decisions in the appropriate meetings. Then people can see that it's not an out-of-control budget, but a well-managed and planned increase in scope or a risk that has become an issue which has driven the change, rather than poor project management on your part.

Keep People Informed

Costs rarely change significantly overnight. For the most part, an increase in project costs will be something that develops over time. Using your information radiators (status reports, steering meetings, project plans etc.) to show how you are tracking against budget is an obvious but sometimes overlooked tool in your toolbox. You might need to put in a checkpoint to drive a discussion about budget if costs have risen significantly over time but keep the surprises to an absolute minimum. Having an agreed trigger, e.g. when the forecast reaches 105% of the original plan, can be a useful way to make it clear to stakeholders that decisions are required on the project.

And Give Them the Decision!

Remember what I said earlier in the book about decisions – Project Managers are in charge of everything except for decisions. Possibly the most important place for you to think like this is when it comes to the costs of the project. If costs are starting to escalate you need to figure out what options and recommendations you are going to give to your stakeholders. This is the time for you to bring out the Iron Triangle that we talked about earlier. You can have it good, you can have it quick, you can have it cheap – pick two!

The iron triangle

This model for deciding on trade-offs is extremely powerful when driving budget discussions. (At least) One of the three elements is going to have to change in response to the changing circumstances of the project, and making an explicit decision on which one will help you understand your stakeholders better as well as giving them control of the big decisions of the project.

If it looks like the timelines are going to be missed, then you can offer your stakeholders to either spend more money getting help or reduce the scope of work that you are all trying to complete. If cost is the problem, then see if there are options to reduce scope (quality) or increase the timelines so that lower-cost team members could be trained and coached to deliver the work over a longer period of time.

By framing the discussion using the Iron Triangle, you take the sting out of the problem and help everyone to focus on working together towards a solution rather than blaming each other for what has gone wrong.

Managing Other Companies

Sometimes the main job of a project manager is managing the other organisations that are delivering part or all of your project. This is where a lot of the stress and much of the conflict comes into poorly managed projects. It is human nature to trust someone who has sold us a solution to deliver that solution on time. However, it is extremely common for those outsourced parts of projects to become the most contentious areas and a lot of time and energy can be wasted in solving disagreement over scope, cost, time, and quality.

Incentives

One of the best ways to think about your vendor relationships is in terms of the incentives that everyone has. If you set up a contract with a vendor where they are paid on a time and materials basis, whereby the more hours they put in, the more they will get paid, then there is a risk that they will opt to do the work in a complicated way to make sure that they get paid as much as possible. If, on the flip side, you are paying for a list of outputs that is agreed up-front before everyone has a good understanding of the project, then you run the risk of having to re-visit the scope as the project progresses and you could easily find yourself in change request purgatory (see Chapter 4). It is also extremely common in a fixed price contract for the buyer not to provide the necessary support to the vendor, because they rely on the vendor to do everything. This also results in a lot more work being done than is necessary. It also often means that vendors include large amounts of padding in their pricing, so you don't get as cost-effective a service as might otherwise be possible.

If pure time and materials are problematic and a fixed price contract also leads to inefficiency, then how should you manage your vendors? The best way to do so is to build trust and control into the relationship, and to do everything you can to align their incentives to those of the project.

Trust comes with the experience of working together and solving problems. While it is inevitable that there will be a contract in place with your vendors, I would recommend only reverting to what is in the contract as an absolute last resort. You are much better off treating your vendor colleagues as part of the team and getting their great ideas on how to achieve the best outcomes for the project.

As we talked about in the discussion regarding agile Vs waterfall projects, most complex projects nowadays are not well understood up-front when you are agreeing the contract with your vendors. This is why I like the concept of including fees at risk and bonuses into contracts in a material way. If you reach a point 3 months into the project where things are going well, and you can give your vendor a bonus for some cost savings that they have found on a different part of the project, then everyone is better off. Likewise, if the vendor knows that they could lose part of their fee if they do not deliver on part of the contract without agreeing on it with you first, then you are starting to align their incentives with yours. This all sounds great in theory, but the rubber hits the road when it comes time to make a fees at risk or bonus decision. This is where you can create an excellent working relationship by being a little bit more generous than you feel you could get away with.

If a vendor messes up (as they almost all do) and expects to get penalised for it, then when you jump on to a call to help them resolve the situation, and then don't penalise them, you have taken a huge step towards building a trusted relationship. If a vendor overperforms and helps you get out of a difficult situation and you give them a generous bonus, then they will look to try and overperform again and again. The key here is to look past the (generally relatively small) costs of paying a bonus, to the (potentially enormous) benefits of having a vendor relationship where everyone is really happy to be working together and has the best interests of the project in mind at all times.

The very best time to open these kinds of discussions with the vendor are right at the start of the project, when they are in "sales" mode, and nothing has gone wrong yet. At this critical point, it is relatively easy to get them to commit in the contract to promises they have made during the sales process. If they say there will be 99.99% uptime of the product, then make sure there is a clause in the contract specifying that if they miss that, they will have to pay back 50% of their monthly fee. If they promise to get the product live in 3 months, then as part of the negotiation on price, make sure that there is €10k "bonus" for hitting that deadline or a €10k fee for missing it.

It is important to realise that there is no difference whatsoever between a €90k fee with a €10k bonus for hitting a deadline and a €100k fee with a €10k penalty for missing the deadline. They are exactly the same thing! If the vendor is unsuccessful in the project, they end up with €90k in both cases. But the difference is that the first one leads to positive conversations about how they can get their bonus, and the second one leads to negative conversations about how they might be charged for failure. Most people don't give bonuses to vendors, but I'd highly recommend thinking about a construct like this at the contract stage.

If you are a savvy negotiator at the contract phase who makes sure that you have levers to pull if and when things go wrong on the project, then you will find managing your vendor much easier when you are deep in the project and struggling to get them to do what you need. Creative negotiation with a view to what could go wrong in the future is rarely time wasted.

Experienced project managers who have had issues with vendors in the past are often able to see the potential pitfalls of the project up-front – in the sales process. This is a valuable skill, as when companies are in sales mode, they like making promises and are confident of their ability to deliver what is being asked of them.

When you are working with a vendor, it's important to see the world from their point of view. They will have other constraints that you can't see – from month and year-end end sales targets to hiring issues and demands from other clients. When you are in negotiating mode, it's great to be able to play these to your advantage – or at least prevent them from becoming a disadvantage at some later point.

Month, Quarter and Year-end

Salespeople are target driven. They get bonuses based on hitting numbers in a certain period. This is a great piece of knowledge as a PM, because it means that you can negotiate for the things you really need and apply a bit of time pressure to the situation. Whether it's a 10% discount, an increase in scope, or a guarantee of access to a certain expert, you can use the end-of-month sales deadline to get things that are valuable to you in return for signing on a specific date.

Creative Negotiation

A lot of people think negotiation is a "zero-sum" game – a high price is bad for the customer, and good for the seller. While this may be true in commodity markets or when you are buying something in a supermarket, it is an absolute fallacy when it comes to buying complicated services. The price is only one factor, and often one of the least important ones. If you have a key partner who is providing a critical part of your project but is only a relatively small part of the overall cost, then you may be much more interested in the timeline or the quality of the service than its price. Being aware of that and building guarantees into the contract negotiation can save you a lot of hassle down the line and make your project go much more smoothly.

It's also important to realise that something which is valuable to you might not be very costly to your counterpart. Or something that is easy for you to provide may be extremely valuable to them. For example, if you are buying a software license that comes in parts, adding an extra module may cost the vendor almost nothing – they simply change a setting in their system, and you have that functionality. On the flip side, many software vendors struggle with getting their clients to test and approve the system or have detailed workshops about how it should be set up. If you can guarantee a 2-hour session every week with your in-house expert, then that can take a lot of effort away from the vendor's team who do not know your company's needs as well as your team do.

These kinds of creative solutions are not at the forefront of many PMs minds during the negotiation, as there is too much focus on price and scope. If you can bring a bit of creativity to the relationship before signing the contract, you will find that it pays dividends later on.

A few other ideas to consider putting on the table when you are negotiating include:

Giving a testimonial or providing a reference for other customers.

- Providing some of your resources to work hand in hand with the vendor resources (e.g. pair programming).
- Hosting a "gemba walk" of the relevant process so that they understand more of the business context.
- Bringing the vendor to Steering meetings to provide updates and seek any help they need.
- Relating vendor bonuses or fees to the success of the project.
- Agreeing on working locations that are helpful to the success of the project – e.g. the vendor team to spend 1 week on site in your company every month throughout the project – or for a couple of your team members to go to the vendors site and work there.
- Payment terms – Could paying immediately for work done rather than waiting 30 or 90 days be valuable to your vendor? (This is particularly powerful with smaller suppliers.).

When Things Go Wrong

In complex projects, where there is uncertainty and volatility over the outcomes, relationships with third parties can sometimes become strained. This is where the relationships and communication that you have built up through the course of the sales process and the project become critical. A lot of PMs revert very quickly to "beating up" on suppliers because it is easier to blame other people than to solve the problem. This is a dangerous game and is the cause of many project failures. If there is a serious issue, it is unlikely to be 100% the fault of the vendor. There are certain things that are within your control which you could have done better.

I encountered a great example of this when I became responsible for an IT operations team who were having huge issues with a supplier of payroll software. The main problem was that the system wasn't stable. Every time there was a software release, defects found their way into the production system which then caused operational problems, delays, and stress. Out of 3 releases before I joined and the first release after I joined, there were "Priority 1" issues every single time we put new code into the live environment. This was despite assurances that both the vendor and the users of the system had comprehensively tested the software before releasing it live.

In this situation, the relationship with the vendor had completely broken down. My predecessor was holding back fees because of the issues, and my new boss was ready to throw away all the work that had been done to put the system in and start again with a different vendor. The credibility of the company was at stake because running payroll was core to the business and our clients were very dissatisfied with all the issues that we were having.

I came into this situation in listening mode, and I started digging into the problem. One of the first things I did was go to lunch with the salesman who had sold us the product in the first place. He was extremely frustrated with the situation because he was confident that the product was a great fit for our business, but we just couldn't seem to get releases in without messing them up. I asked him the killer question – that no one else in my company had thought to ask him – what did he think **we** were doing wrong?

That one question changed the dynamic of the whole conversation. Instead of blaming each other and having frustrated conversations under pressure when there were live issues, we were able to figure out a plan to resolve the situation very effectively. There were a few issues which were causing the trouble.

- While they were a leader in this type of software for the UK market, there were some differences in the way tax calculations were done in Ireland which always caused problems.
- They did not really understand how we were using the system, and the training programme that was supposed to have happened for our team had not been completed because of the live issues.
- Their testing focused on scenarios relevant to the UK market but did not cover all the different scenarios relevant to Ireland.
- Our testing was being done by busy operations people, who were trying to fit it in around their day jobs.

Once we'd had this conversation, there were a few things that we were able to do which completely changed the whole situation.

- We hired a full-time tester whose job was to get to know both our business and the system and put a lot more formality around our testing.
- We introduced the software company to the Irish Tax Authorities and facilitated a much more proactive relationship between the two organisations, including getting them access to a testing environment which mirrored the live environment they had to interface with.
- We went over to see them in their offices and explained our business to them, and how our operations worked.
- They came over to our offices and worked together with our operations team to understand how processes needed to work and explain how the system should be used.

Within a few months, we had completely turned the situation around. Releases stopped having so many issues. Known defects started getting fixed, and the two teams started working much more closely together. They even started to socialise together on the visits between the two offices. From staring down the barrel of having to undertake a massive project to replace the whole payroll system from scratch, we were able to resolve all the issues and build a great relationship which cost us a fraction of the time and effort that replacing the system would have cost.

All of this came from switching from a "blame culture" with the vendor to a "partnership culture", and over time the trust came back, and the product became one of the most stable and trusted systems in our estate.

The moral of the story – as a Project Manager, it doesn't matter whose fault an issue is, it is your responsibility to fix it. And once you take that responsibility on and work proactively to resolve all the issues, your project is much more likely to be a success.

Having the right approach to contingency, managing your team and resources using the high value/ low effort matrix, and negotiating successful agreements with your vendors will go a long way to helping you manage project costs with impact. Alongside what you have already learned about estimating and having great conversations with your stakeholders around the uncertainty of the future, hopefully this chapter has provided plenty of food for thought about how you are managing the costs of your project to ensure that it is delivering successfully on its business goals.

Chapter 12
Conclusion – Project Management Can Be Better

Impactful project managers control the flow of work and make sure it is all valuable

Project management can be hard. It can be stressful and draining and it can take over your life. You will feel pressure from stakeholders, you will miss deadlines, you will come across unforeseen issues, and you will get many, many things wrong.

It can also be an enormously rewarding career. For the right person with the right skills, it is a challenging and satisfying way to spend your time. There will be new scenarios to face every day, different problems to solve, and different people to meet. No two projects are the same, and most project managers will find variety and diversity in their choice of career.

We have touched on a lot of themes throughout this book. We have deliberately focused on practical tips and approaches rather than theory. You now understand the lenses that you need to look through when it comes to project management, as well as many different techniques to use that you can make your own. This toolbox should give you the power to be impactful as a project manager, but I'd like to finish with a few more general points that might help as well.

Having discussed these topics with hundreds of project managers over the years, there are three levers that I've found to be highly effective as people think about managing their projects. These are more general themes that people tend to get the balance a little bit wrong on, and that might just trigger a few final ideas for your own project before you put this book down.

https://doi.org/10.1515/9783111271149-012

Transparency

Being confident about how you are managing your project is something that comes with time. Some people have had bad experiences in the past with sharing their work and it being "picked apart" by more senior colleagues. They tend to keep their work to themselves unless asked for it. This is a shame, because it leaves a huge amount of improvement both in terms of learning and outcomes on the table.

There is a point that many successful people reach in their careers where a switch flips in their head. Instead of being worried about feedback, they start to seek it out. They start to discuss their approaches with colleagues, not looking for validation that they have done a good job, but criticism and improvement of the approach they are taking. The earlier this switch flips for you, the more you will learn, and the better you will get.

So how do you get into this mindset? It's simple – share your working! Be transparent about what is going on, be confident in the approaches that you are taking, but not so arrogant that you think they can't be improved. A problem shared is a problem halved, and being open and transparent about what you and your team are doing will create a confidence that is hard to beat.

It's also very simple to do. Ask for suggestions and feedback on your plan or risk log, publish your status report on the company intranet, or send out a communication to your stakeholders asking for their help on a thorny problem. Over time, this transparency will raise your profile, and the profile of your project. You are more likely to get the help you need, but you will also hear about great career opportunities for yourself and your team. People will start coming to you for advice, and they will ask you to take on bigger and more important pieces of work because they see that you are managing things well. It can be a little uncomfortable at first as the rough edges are knocked off your presentations and style, but in time, your career and stress levels will both benefit from adding a bit more transparency to what you are doing.

This theme of transparency is especially valuable when it comes to the risks to your project. By holding a SAVE workshop (see Chapter 3) with your team to identify Risks, and then using Planning Poker to estimate the contingency needed for each one, you can make the reality of your project much more transparent. Using these risks and contingency estimates, you can then have amazing, transparent discussions with your stakeholders about the cost, scope, and timelines of your project and help them to make the best decisions possible to drive really positive outcomes for your business.

Prioritisation

I have talked a lot about prioritisation throughout this book because it is the one area where I think most people can benefit a lot from quite a small shift in mindset. I'm not alone. Many of the self-help books that you might read will talk about things like valuing your own time, saying no to things, intentionality, and choosing how you spend your time effectively. These are all different ways of saying that you should make active decisions about how you and your team spend your time.

Allowing low value / high effort work to creep into your project (or your life) is one of the most damaging and stressful things you can do. It will sap your energy and enthusiasm, tire you out, and prevent you from achieving the impact that you want to achieve.

Prioritization starts with knowing **why** you are doing something. Aligning it to an important goal and making sure that it will make a positive impact on that goal is crucial, but don't stop there. You should also look to make sure that there aren't any even more effective ways of achieving that and other goals. Remember Baloo's advice – look for the papaws and avoid the prickly pears!

Humanity

The world is changing at an incredible pace. Tools like generative AI, process automation, and the way we use data to make decisions will disrupt all our lives. The connections we have to people are under attack from remote and flexible work, the gig economy, changes in the way we communicate, social media, and the constant war for our attention. These are all good things in their own way, they have great benefits, but they will erode the human connection you have with your colleagues. As an impactful project manager, any way that you can ramp up the humanity in your team or with your stakeholders will be crucial for your success in the future.

This will not be easy. Asking people to commute to the office just to have "face time" together will meet with push-back for many good reasons. Having personal conversations is much harder on group video calls than in a face-to-face meeting where side-bar chats can break out organically and continue afterwards. Getting people to speak to each other when it is so easy to just send a Slack or Teams message can be monumentally challenging.

But it is your job to make sure that your team are happy, healthy, and working well together. No one else is going to take responsibility for it, and without the human connection, stress and a lack of support can have a real impact on people's mental health and their ability to be effective. There are a few things that you can do to add this humanity every day.

- Check in with people. Face-to-face, if possible, but online if necessary. Simply grabbing a coffee, shooting the breeze, asking how someone is doing, and then really listening to the answer is a simple but often overlooked activity for overly busy project managers.
- Make face-time count! Don't bring people into the office just to sit next to each other on Zoom calls. Bring them in for specific, high Impact events.
  - A collaborative workshop using Silent Writing and Affinity Clustering, or Lean Coffee will enable people to be heard and get value from being together face-to-face.
  - A mentoring or reverse-mentoring programme will give team members an excuse to get together.
  - A specific problem-solving session on one of your biggest problems can show how important it is for people to get together.
  - Training sessions or "Lunch N Learn" can be a great reason to get people together.
  - Performance reviews and 1:1s are best done face to face; maybe they should be a bit more regular than once per year?
  - Meeting a third party or other vendor gives a good focus for people to get together face-to-face.
  - What about a "Town Hall" with a senior executive coming to meet the team to explain the context of the project and what is going on in the wider organisation?
  - Saying thank you and having some fun. Spending a bit of money on a team activity or a few drinks or dinner is much more important now than it was just a few years ago. Give people a great reason to get together and relax and you will find that they work much more effectively together, and with a lot less stress for the next few weeks.

But humanity isn't just the big stuff. Tell a bad "dad joke," share a picture of what you did at the weekend, and ask people for a recommendation of something to watch on the television. By demonstrating these kinds of behaviours, yourself, you will help set the culture of your team to do the same. Leadership is not telling people what to do; it's showing them how and helping them to do it.

What I have tried to do in this book is to give you a set of tools that you can use to make your project management career more successful. These tools and approaches are important because they drive real behaviour. Project management is a proactive, energetic activity. Understanding why you are doing things and making sure that the things you are doing are valuable and effective sounds simple, but it can be hard. With these tips and techniques, hopefully it will be a little easier in the future, and you and your team can have a bit more fun being highly impactful.

There is a responsibility on all managers to use their skills and knowledge to support those around them. You have enormous influence over your colleagues, the levels of pressure they feel, the opportunities they get, and the stress that they are under. However you have seen project management in the past I hope that you will look to the future with positivity and excitement. You can make an enormous positive impact on how people feel about their work, and themselves and their success in project after project. I hope you have a great time doing it, and I wish you every success in your future projects.

Ongoing Learning

As you know, I love post-it notes, so at the end of my live training I ask everyone for feedback on the course. Here is what they said after the very first session:

> "A high energy and interactive course."
>
> "The course challenged me to think differently about managing projects and people."
>
> "James is a brilliant facilitator. This course can be applied to any job role."
>
> "No-nonsense, practical techniques delivered in a high-energy and engaging course."
>
> "Energetic + Good practical tools for all PMs."
>
> "I loved the HiPPO concept."
>
> "Without doubt one of the best training courses I have ever attended in every discipline."
>
> "James' delivery style was very engaging throughout the 2 days."
>
> "A useful reminder on key project management skills with brilliant tips and observations from real-world experience."
>
> "Great for problem solving."

Hopefully you feel the same way about the book that you have just read. Whether you do or not, I'd be very grateful if you would leave a review wherever you bought it from, so I can see if it's hit the right notes for my future work.

If you would like to keep learning more about these subjects, I have set up an online community to support project managers who want to share ideas and continue learning. On there you will find my full 2-day flagship training course, as well as a host of other curated content, a book club, Q&A, masterclasses, live events and much more.

https://www.impactfulpm.com/ireadthebook

Use the code IREADTHEBOOK for a special discount to get you started.
(If you want an even better discount, you can use the code ILEFTAREVIEW 😉)

https://doi.org/10.1515/9783111271149-013

Do You Disagree with Anything in this Book?

I love to learn!

If you disagree with anything in this book or have ideas on how things could be explained in a different way, please reach out to me on LinkedIn (https://www.linkedin.com/in/james-louttit) or email james@impactfulpm.com

Bulk Orders, Training and Speaking

Some of my clients like to use this book as a gift and training aid for their management teams. If you would like to order bulk copies of this book, or arrange for training, consultancy or speaking engagements, please email james@impactfulpm.com or stefan.giesen@degruyter.com or go to https://www.degruyter.com/document/isbn/9783111271149/html

https://doi.org/10.1515/9783111271149-014

About the Author

James Louttit runs Impactful Project Management, which provides training based on 20 years' experience delivering projects and coaching others. He has taken on many roles in project delivery from business analysis, coding and testing through to project and programme management, and leadership positions as Project Management Competency Lead at Bank of Ireland and Chief Information Officer at Cpl, before founding Impactful Project Management in January 2023. In November 2023, James's approach to humanising project management training was recognised when he won the prestigious "Project Management Professional of the Year" award from the Ireland Chapter of the Project Management Institute.

He has taught project management principles to hundreds of people from all backgrounds and levels of experience. His innovative, human style using stories, cartoons, vlogs, games and discussion to explain complex ideas is popular in conferences, corporate events and across a range of social media and traditional media formats.

James studied politics, philosophy and economics at Oxford and brings the insights from these fields and many others into his understanding of project management to give a stimulating, refreshing, sometimes controversial perspective that is valuable to new project managers and old hands alike.

James lives in Dublin with his family where he is very active in the local community, as a leader in the scout group, building DIY projects and staying playful with his three young children.

https://doi.org/10.1515/9783111271149-015

About the Illustrator

Tais Krymova has been drawing since childhood. Her favourite subjects have always been animals and people in different styles. But most of all she loves drawing in realistic style, cartoon style, and combining the two.

"I do love working with James because his needs match my talents very well. We started this project before the full-scale invasion of Ukraine started, but even this big problem couldn't stop us . . . I believe the book will be useful to every reader!"

https://doi.org/10.1515/9783111271149-016

List of Illustrations

https://doi.org/10.1515/9783111271149-017

Index

https://doi.org/10.1515/9783111271149-018